Crisis Points

Editors: Ian Taylor and Jock Young

The impact of the last five years of economic and political crisis in Britain appears to have dulled the nerve and commitment of the 'informed' political and social critic. 'Inevitable progress', 'benign capitalism', 'the politics of consensus' – the clichés of the sixties are still paraded as the conventional wisdom of the seventies. One consequence of this has been a dearth of informed and incisive discussion of issues such as the decline of educational, health and welfare services, the impact of inflation on living standards, physical fitness and nutrition and the everyday experience of poverty, illness, racism and crime in present-day Britain. This series focuses on the erosion of both the social and the political rights of the individual: for the decline in living standards is mirrored by the threat of new legislation and police powers to the freedom of the individual. Such a tightening of the reins of control has its cultural manifestation whether it is in the appearance of a new McCarthyism in the media and the universities or in the signs of resistance in youth culture and the new wave of popular music.

The Crisis Points series aims to rectify this gap in contemporary debate. The books are written from the inside by practitioners or activists confronting the crisis in their field of work; they are informed in their content not academic in their style; and they are accessible to the increasing numbers of the public concerned with the social problems of our times. Above all they are short and provocative – a basis of debate, whether it be in the home, classroom or workplace.

Health in Danger

The Crisis in the National
Health Service

David Widgery

M

© David Widgery 1979

All rights reserved. No part of this publication
may be reproduced or transmitted, in any form
or by any means, without permission.

First published 1979 by
THE MACMILLAN PRESS LTD
London and Basingstoke
Associated companies in Delhi Dublin
Hong Kong Johannesburg Lagos Melbourne
New York Singapore and Tokyo

Printed by A. Wheaton & Co., Ltd., Exeter

British Library Cataloguing in Publication Data

Widgery, David
  Health in danger. – (Crisis points).
  1. Great Britain – National Health Service
  I. Title II. Series
  362.1′0941   RA395.G6

  ISBN 0–333–23025–6
  ISBN 0–333–23178–3 Pbk.

A Worker's Speech to a Doctor

We know what makes us ill.
When we are ill we are told
That it's you who will heal us.

For ten years, we are told
You learned healing in fine schools
Built at the people's expense
And to get your knowledge
Spent a fortune.
So you must be able to heal.

Are you able to heal?
When we come to you
Our rags are torn off us
And you listen all over our naked body.
As to the cause of our illness
One glance at our rags would
Tell you more. It is the same cause that wears out
Our bodies and our clothes.

The pain in our shoulder comes
You say, from the damp; and this is also the reason
For the stain on the wall of our flat.
So tell us:
Where does the damp come from?

Too much work and too little food
Makes us feeble and thin.
Your prescription says:
Put on more weight.
You might as well tell a bullrush
Not to get wet.

How much time can you give us?
We see: one carpet in your flat costs
The fees you earn from
Five thousand consultations.

You'll no doubt say
You are innocent. The damp patch
On the walls of our flats
Tells the same story.

Bertolt Brecht

To Ruth

Contents

Acknowledgements

To the Royal Free, the suffragette's medical school, and to Dr Frances Gardner, for teaching me medicine, to Drs Sherlock, McIntyre and Bouchier for inspiring me about medicine and to Dr Michael Leibson and the people of Bethnal Green for being down to earth about it.

Thanks to the International Socialists and the East London Hospitals Branch of the Socialist Workers Party, especially Wendy, Steve and John, for teaching me about politics. Thanks to the British Museum, the Nuffield Library of the British Medical Association, the *Hospital Worker* and the Montague Road Archives for books. Thanks to Dave for lending his room and sorry for throwing Jayne's spinach and cheese pastry rolls around. Remember to read the *Hospital Worker*. Thanks to the *Radio Times*, the *International Journal of Health Services*, *International Socialism* and *Socialist Worker* for space to try out early drafts. Thanks to Juliet for staying sane and to Val Clarke for typing, editing and inquiring.

The author and publishers wish to thank Eyre Methuen Ltd for permission to include the poem 'A Worker's Speech to a Doctor' by Bertolt Brecht, translated by Frank Jellinek, from *Poems 1913–1956*, edited by John Willett and Ralph Manheim. Copyright in the original 'Svendborger Gedichte' © 1939 by Malik-Verlag, London. Translation copyright © 1976 by Eyre Methuen Ltd.

Introduction

Practicing as a doctor did not turn out quite as predicted at medical school. In this era of cuts and economic crisis it can be something of a nightmare: a morning surgery; repeat prescriptions of drugs that do not work; repeat visits for depression I cannot cure; diets low in nutrition; lives emptied of relaxation; the social worker's telephone will not answer; the drug company representative wastes precious time; blood tests are being centralised, so fail to arrive; the twenty waiting patients grow impatient. The scrupulous methods taught at medical school collapse under the pressure. Instead you do the best you can in the circumstances and pray that mistakes will be avoided.

I make the visits through dirty streets blowing with litter and pounded by gigantic lorries. Because lifts are out of order, I go up damp stairways etched with hateful graffiti. Homes are warm and crowded, embarrassingly grateful: tears and biscuits and processed cheese; after a hour on the telephone, the ambulance is on its way. On the way home, late for lunch as always, a man in his twenties is working his way through a dustbin, looking for something to eat, an Asian clothing worker glues his eyes to the gutter as schoolchildren jeer at him. In the post a new mound of area plans which, when deciphered, reveals that the local hospital where I did my house-jobs, is to close; a note from the Elizabeth Garrett Anderson Hospital, where I learnt some of my gynaecology; the hospital occupation committee calls on its supporters for one further show of strength.

A bad day, we all have them. Perhaps things will go smoothly tomorrow. It only becomes a crazy day when I turn on the televised party conference and see a Labour Prime Minister, with insincere smiles and mixed metaphors, telling his party that everything is going splendidly. The practice senior has worked in East London for thirty years. 'You're learning,' he says. 'Still hang on to those socialist dreams?'. This book comes out of messy days like that. It is an attempt to unravel quite what is happening to our health service and explain its implications to the public who rely on it. It's also an attempt to restate the socialist case for comprehensive and democratic health care. And in the process it is an attack on the public spending cuts enforced so vigilantly by the Callaghan administration.

This is not an easy time to advance principles about the health service, but that service would never have come into existence if those principles had not existed in the minds of tens of thousands. 'The party's over,' say the realists. 'We will simply have to lower our sights.' 'It makes the best of a bad job', says the administrator about his plan. It reminds me of the Brecht poem: 'Those who eat their full, speak to the hungry about the wonderful times to come. Those who lead the country into the abyss, call ruling too difficult for ordinary men.' If our local hospital closes, its 240 beds and 38,000 casualty and out-patient visitors will simply have to join the lengthy queues at the remaining hard-pressed hospital. But the administrators who will carry out the gutting, and the government which instructs them, say, as they stride into the abyss, the public does not seem to understand the issues clearly. In the face of their crackpot realism, you do start to wonder if we, the nurses, doctors, laundry workers and local people who protest are really unhinged extremists?

I think not. And that those ordinary rank-and-file people who have resisted the closures will eventually be seen as wise and honourable, just as we now see the unpopular and isolated pioneers of public-health measures as the clear-sighted ones. And when the full effects of the cuts are revealed, the policy will be seen as perhaps the final turn in the Labour Party's journey from the party of post-war social-democratic optimism to the party of social authority, the iron-handed and hard-hearted champion of the needs of the capitalist economy. The N. H. S. was once the centrepiece of the Labour Dream. Now that party has new mottos: 'Soak the Poor', 'Sod the Sick', 'Bash the Firemen' and 'All Power to the I. M. F.' It has not merely neglected the N. H. S., it has forced it into mediocrity, all the time like a political Canute insisting that everything is still rosy even as the waves overwhelm it.

This is why the first part of the book seeks to sketch out the origins of the public-health service and show how every advance has come through a productive conflict between the iron laws of finance and the social needs of the people. Health has always been too expensive. Those sleek administrators who insist on closing working services have their forerunners in the tight-fisted Poor Law Guardians and the complacent Gradgrinds. And if Wakley, the founder of the *Lancet* were to be reborn, he would at once take up his pen against the self-enriching drug empires and dishonest Ministers, for he understood that parsimony and neglect would be inevitable as long as conditions inside the health service were kept a private matter, of no interest to the healthy.

No one is suggesting we have returned to Poor Law conditions, but a Poor Law mentality is certainly abroad again. And it thrives on ignorance. If the general public were fully aware of the degree of the decline in standards in parts of the N. H. S., I am quite convinced they would demand a halt in the cuts. 'No government,' wrote Aneurin Bevan, 'that attempts to destroy the N. H. S. can hope to command the support of the British people.' The settlement of 1949 had many flaws and compromises, some of which have inevitably become inflamed again; but it did seem to guarantee a framework of steady improvement. Its buildings may have been ancient but morale was buoyed up by promises: a new nuclear hospital, the long-promised health centre, an extra staff member to share the inhuman hours of compulsory overtime. Now those hopes are over. In the present era, everything has gone into reverse gear. New building is postponed indefinitely, new hospitals at Sheffield, Oxford and Leicester cannot open, general practice is beginning to break down in some city areas, staff levels shrink. Sensible plans for rationalisation are rushed through at such a speed that consultation is discredited, staff made cynical and hospitals which, with imagination, could find an altered role are swept out with the bath-water. So far the most dramatic cuts have been in London and Liverpool but now that the framework is established, areas initially protected will feel the gnawing of the cuts, and the decline in morale when everything is stamped with the cuts mentality. The Conservative Party waits in the wings with even more Draconian policies: abolition of health centres, reintroduction of health insurance, and fees for hospital admission and home visiting by doctors.

It is to be hoped that informed public opposition will become more vocal. Senior doctors are finally overcoming their professional and temperamental dislike of publicity to comment publicly on the damage to medical standards. Medical scandals such as the report on conditions in Friern Barnet Mental Hospital or the new Barnsley District General, thanks to people like Eric Moonman M. P. and Mr Sharad Mahatme, will no longer be covered over. Surgeons like Leon

Abrams and David Clarke of Queen Elizabeth Hospital, Birmingham, after months of unanswered correspondence with the Minister are now prepared to expose publicly the fact that, with an average delay for cardiac surgery of six months, one acutely ill patient dies every month awaiting admission. 'It's a terrible comment on the health service that non-urgent cases are rarely operated on until they deteriorate and then become urgent', said Abrams in February 1978. Public shock about such operations as the forced closure of Hounslow Hospital grows faster than is realised by an obstinate Ministry. Things are going badly wrong when such unlikely militants as the sisters at Hounslow lead a work-in and the authorities organise a late-night raid with a fleet of private ambulances and strong-arm men to ward off crying nurses and dismantle furniture to prevent its further use. And, as resistance grows, the Minister will need more and more forced and violent closures, of the quietly determined Plaistow Maternity Hospital, of the Bethnal Green Hospital and of others whose names we do not yet know. Mr Ennals will find them not so easily caught napping, with better established lines of union and community support. 'Enough,' as the East London campaigners say, 'is enough.'

So far resistance has been piecemeal, mosaic-like, poorly co-ordinated. Much official union protest has smacked of going through the motions, channelling resistance into general formal protest with little real impact, shadow-boxing in the corridors of power rather than in active effective local defence. The most glaring example of this was the deafening silence from the hospital union leaders in the days after the Hounslow raid, when hospital workers *were* ready for a really massive protest, lest it detract from their own arbitrary, expensive and ineffective week of protest, which duly went off like a sodden squib. Instead it has been left to the informal unofficial rank-and-file union networks, the 'Right to Work' campaigners, the small left-wing groups like the much-reviled Socialist Workers Party, the Women's Liberation supporters, the cranks, the dreamers and the amateurs to piece together resistance. According to the official politicians, these people are extremists, for the mainstream parties both agree about cuts and simply argue about their degree. But I have met more determined extremists and enforcers of minority views in the corridors of hospital-management power than in the responsible, makeshift and unpaid anti-cuts committees. Indeed, a society which flies empty Concordes to Bahrein 'loses' £200 million at its Crown Agents and puts 3000 nurses on the dole to 'stimulate manufacturing industry' has more topsy-turvy values than those local groups of anti-cuts campaigners who simply want their hospitals to stay open.

But resisting the cuts means a larger battle to reverse some of the crackpot priorities of modern Britain and shape a society based on human values of the sort Bevan described so eloquently and the modern Labour Party has forgotten so completely; for the cuts mentality affects education, housing and social welfare and is no longer simply a piece of government budgeting but the codeword for a social counter-revolution.

Students of political economy will recognise the cuts as an aspect of the larger problem of British capitalism in raising the level of productivity in its service sector.

We are entering a dismal new world and a society which is far crueller and meaner. It will have a million-strong army of per-manently workless, its great public corporations of transport and power will now be run for profit, its educational system wrenched round to fit the exact needs of industry, its 'social security' insecure and anti-social. It will see the end of cheap food, of cheap anything, and the beginning of charges for everything. Common humanity becomes too expensive and, as always, it is those most in need who are the first to suffer, those who have the least who have the most taken away. We tend to see economic depression in images of the past, of Jarrow and hunger marchers, not noticing the suffering under our noses because we cannot see it for the television commercials and party political broadcasts. But the crisis in the N. H. S. is part of a much larger collapse in the Welfare State and the whole body of post-war liberal and Fabian social thought which took full employment and rising wages for granted. The social scientists have yet to measure its statistics, but the cold who have their meters cut off, the sick in search of a hospital, the jobless school-leavers, the claimants who endure insulting rules, endless waiting and humiliating cross-questioning – the human statistics – know what is happening.

I had to write this book because I do care what happens to the N. H. S. and I do not want to see its best idealism and inspiration squandered by Treasury accountants. I am part of the generation shaped by Beveridge and Bevan; I got the chance to train as a doctor because of post-war educational reform and the grammar schools; I survived childhood illness in N. H. S. hospitals; I know what even those quite modest reforms have meant to the quality of people's lives their health and their human development. I cannot sit quietly while it is dismantled before my eyes, and while children, no different from me fifteen years ago, now leave school with no future.

After being involved in political campaigning for years, one becomes a little numbed to even one's own arguments. So it was almost with surprise I realised this summer quite how much I cared about the future of the N. H. S. I was in a hill-top chapel, high over the slums of Palermo, which has been ravaged by several polio epidemics. Inside the chapel was the Sicilian alternative to a health service. They relied instead on the power of prayer. The statue of the patron Saint Theresa was festooned with the limbs of plastic dolls, each one symbolising the withered part of a loved one. Outside the chapel stall-owners sold tawdry mascots and religious paraphenalia. In reality prayer did nothing except enrich the priests on the hill, while the polio victims begged, stole or died in the alleys below. Turning in to my English airmail copy of the *Guardian* for a breath of liberality, I read a news item: 'A facelift worth £1000 carried out by a top Harley Street surgeon is top prize in a raffle for high society guests at a special ball in the Dorchester Hotel.' Both were sickening but the Dorchester Hotel incident more so. Both were about the barbarism of societies where good health is not a right but a prize in some unearthly lottery, societies where health is unequal because power and wealth are distributed unequally. I, too, caught polio badly in the 1956 epidemic. Through the N. H. S. I spent five years having a series of reconstructive operations which largely removed the crippling effect of the disease. Over those painful five years I graduated from wheelchair and callipers to my first pair of shop-bought shoes. My parents could never have afforded that surgery in a private health service, an insurance-based system would never cover it, I am doubtful about Saint Theresa's ability to deliver the goods, and the Dorchester's not my style. Yet the cuts threaten exactly that kind of surgery which ought to be available on the N. H. S. without question but which can be done without. John Sherrard, the consultant orthopaedic surgeon at Sheffield Children's Hospital, has stated that because of staff shortages in the Sheffield area 'Spastic children will have their hips go out of date so that they will never be able to walk, children who remain ugly through curvature of the spine will get progressively worse and look twice as ugly, and others cannot go to school because they cannot wear shoes.'

My own life, as much as my politics, tell me that the level of compassion with which a society treats its sick and crippled, its old and its feeble-minded is the real measure of that society's level of civilisation. It tells me that we need a society arranged around enjoyed good health rather than a health service snuffling after disease like a baffled bloodhound. It tells me the N. H.S. has not failed but that we have not given it a real chance. This book will have been worth writing if it convinces more people that it is something worth fighting for.

Christmas 1977   DAVID WIDGERY

1
The early hospitals

Only 130 years ago, Sir John Simon, perhaps the nineteenth century's most shrewd, eminent and unpopular physician, described the state of medical knowledge as scarcely beyond 'nurses' gossip and sick men's fancies and the crude compilations of a blundering empiricism'. Doctors were still examined on their Latin rather than their anatomy, and judged by their attire more than their application. The clinical thermometer and the stethoscope were still novelties, and the microscope's use had to be defended. Medicine was poised on the brink of a scientific breakthrough but was still shrouded in superstition. Hospitals, far from offering succour to the sick, were dreaded. 'The first requirement in a hospital,' wrote Florence Nightingale, 'is that it should do the sick no harm', and on that criterion alone the early hospitals failed.

The rich endured their treatment in their homes, selecting their physicians from the Royal Colleges on the basis of snobbery, nepotism or their man's reputation in the voluntary hospitals, where aspiring doctors would quite literally practise on the poor. The middling classes would be more likely to depend on an apothecary, qualified by a five-year apprenticeship in a pharmacy and able to charge for medicine supplied but not for medical advice. For the rest there were the quacks, estimated in Lincolnshire in 1864 to outnumber the trained men by a ratio of nine to one.[1]

Women, systematically excluded from the profitable business of doctoring, as servants or relatives 'watched' the sick, assisted with traditional remedies, delivered the new born, and laid out the dead. Death was so commonplace, disease so mysterious and suffering so natural that illness itself was best explained as the earthly evidence of divine displeasure. In the midst of such ignorance the priest was able to exercise his piety and the quack to extract his pence.

In 1819 the atheist bookseller, Richard Carlile, wrote in disgust to his own doctor about the virtues of the old female herbalists:

All you knew was that professional men thought proper to disguise their medicines and not let their patients know what they had swallowed. You knew nothing of the chemical qualities of mercury; you had learnt to mix it up for different purposes as a medicine, just as your wiser medical predecessors, the old women, had learnt to administer herbs and to repeat prayers as charms. Like those old ladies, with you it was hit and miss, every case an experiment; if the patient is killed, the fault is in the disease; if he recovers, wonderfully clever doctor! There is much less chance of being killed by an old lady for a doctress, as she will not be so rash with her experiments, preferring her herbs to minerals crude and calcinated. Your whole administration of drugs, or what you call physic, or medicine, is a system of guess work. The bases of the human body you do not study . . . you first learn to read gallipot Latin, then to mix different drugs, and to act as barber surgeons. Next you are off to London, to have a *walk through the hospitals*, as it is termed, and with many of you it is a mere walk. You enter your names to attend certain courses of lectures as students, and whether you attend or not, you find no difficulty in getting your certificate of qualification.[2]

In 1823 the first edition of the radically minded medical journal the *Lancet* announced:

We hope the age of 'Mental Delusion' has passed and that mystery and concealment will no longer be encouraged. Indeed we trust that mystery and ignorance will shortly be considered synonymous. Ceremonies and signs have now lost their charm, hieroglyphics and serpents their power to deceive.

But when the *Lancet*'s first editor, Wakley – coroner, M. P., scourge of the quacks and critic of the apothecaries – collapsed from exhaustion twenty-nine years later, scientific medicine was still struggling to find its feet. Remedies could be bought or remembered, but when they failed, when there were no relatives to help, when sickness had made them penniless or poverty had made them ill, patients would be forced into institutional medical care – either in the voluntary hospitals or in the workhouses.

Voluntary hospitals

The pioneer hospitals like St Bart's and St Thomas's have their origins in medieval religious charity, but most of the voluntary hospitals were founded by civic or royal initiative in the eighteenth century. By 1800 there were forty such hospitals providing 4000 beds: even allowing for the much smaller population, only 1/25 of present-day provision. Although the hospital movement clearly betokened a willingness by the rich to ease the sufferings of the sick poor, it was not without self-interest. Becoming a hospital governor was one of the routes for the rising merchant to enter the social elite. It enabled entry into an exclusive world of fêtes and bazaars where, in the name of charity, the newly enriched encountered the nobility. Some governors had a direct financial interest in supplying the hospitals and all subscribers were entitled to nominate prospective patients by providing them with a Letter of Introduction.

The distinguished doctors who walked the hospital wards with such commotion gave their services without charge. But their honorary service in the public hospitals was a species of self-advertisement for their private practice, where their clients would include many of the governors themselves. Day-to-day medical supervision would be carried out by their students and juniors, with a mixture of resentment and self-abasement. The senior men, having made a slow and patient passage to the pinnacle of their profession and the apogee of public esteem, were understandably reluctant to share the spoils. The teaching element in the voluntary hospitals grew steadily in importance. It became an important source of the senior doctors' income, not least from the referrals made by ex-pupils once qualified. The voluntary hospitals were an ideal supply of human material for teaching and research. The paupers in receipt of charity were by reason of their wretched financial and social standing debarred from objecting to being pinched, pummelled and percussed by the legion of students who walked behind the great physicians. Charity had a way of reducing the recipient to the exact degree it enhanced the donor.

The patients, by imploring a 'ticket' from a subscriber and bribing a steward into the bargain, gained entry into a harsh world. Medical attention was brief and haphazard, depending more on the novelty of the affliction than the severity of the condition. Nurses worked very long hours with no set periods for time off, and traditionally passed the night by the good offices of the gin bottle (although some were undoubtedly more experienced healers than the doctors). The wards were unhygienic and poorly divided, so cross-infection must have been rife. Food was dull and contained little nourishment, and was sometimes itself grubby and infested. Separation of contagious skin and fever patients was uncommon and they were sometimes excluded from hospital altogether, with the result that those most in need of isolation stayed free to dispense infection. The consultants' desire to impress the world with their curative powers led them to select patients with diseases in which visible improvement was likely to be swiftly registered. The other side of that coin was an effective bar on the admission of the chronically sick, the old and the very poor, who then, as now, are unpopular among doctors because medical measures alone do not produce dramatic improvements. These people were shuttled to the tender mercies of the workhouses, whose patients exceeded in number the sick in the voluntary hospitals. Their lot was still more miserable.

Workhouse infirmaries

Since Elizabethan days, the Poor Law system had provided rudimentary relief for the poor. Poverty was a constant and, so the rich thought, a necessary presence in most people's lives. Low wages, seasonal work and trade depressions made saving impossible, and death, disease or simply passing of the years could turn a once diligent worker over to the mercies of the parish. The able-bodied artisan only avoided relief by the earnings of children, assistance from friends and loans from traders, and all three were strictly limited. The grim workhouses kept costs to a minimum by confining all the needy in one dwelling, unsatisfactory for most purposes but especially so for use as a hospital. Just as the pinch of the workhouse was thought to inspire the labouring poor to work, so the starkness of medical care was expected to reveal imposters or provide an appropriate place to die for those whose illness proved genuine but who lacked strength to labour. 'Our intention,' said one Assistant Commissioner, 'is to make the workhouse as like prison as possible', and another: 'our object . . . is to establish a discipline so severe and repulsive as to make them a terror to the poor and prevent them from entering.'[3] This deliberate punishment of the poor and sick was intensified as a result of the 1832–4 Poor Law Commissioners' Report and the legislation it prompted. Chadwick's skilfully biased report succeeded in establishing the principle of 'less eligibility'. Poor relief was to be made deliberately unpleasant, should only be provided within workhouses and was to be consciously cruel, tight-fisted and humiliating. The intention was to separate the workshy from the genuinely destitute by cutting off all 'out-door' relief to the able-bodied in temporary need.

'Less eligible'

The social philosophy behind this sadism was that poverty and unemployment were healthy and natural events which strengthened the moral fibre. Pauperism or the state of being poor was a great evil due to moral defects: a dislike of labour or a proclivity for strong drink. Unchecked pauperism might lead to desperate uprisings against authority, or worse infect the honest working man with dissent. As the always canny Chadwick put it, 'if a Chartist millenium is to be averted, the governing classes must free the governed from the sharp spur of their misery by improving the physical conditions of their lives'.[4] It was therefore politically necessary as well as morally and administratively convenient to greatly expand workhouse build-ings, or 'Bastilles', as the poor ungraciously dubbed them, in memory of the terrible Parisian prison thrown open in the Revolution, as long as they provided such dismal conditions as the considerable ingenuity of the Guardians could devise.

Strictly speaking the sick were excluded from the 'less eligible' test and were entitled to be treated at home. Nevertheless they accumu-lated steadily until by 1861 a total of 50,000 were under the care of workhouse medical officers, many shuttled into the Poor Law after the voluntary hospitals had despaired of curing them and become embarrassed by their presence.

The medical officers were selected mainly on their willingness to make do with very low wages. They were expected to provide medicines out of their tiny salaries, which guaranteed parsimony in prescribing. Trained staff were scanty. Nursing was often carried out on a cost-free basis by the paupers themselves. The doctors were inferior in rank and status to the workhouse masters, whose overriding aim was to keep costs to a minimum, and who were more anxious to prevent imagined abuse than to cure the poor. The beadle, and *then* the doctor, examined the sick. It was the Poor Law service which accommodated the bulk of sick children, mental cases, skin conditions, epileptics, diabetics, patients infected with tuberculosis, syphilis and scarlet fever, and the undiagnosed and probably unexamined thousands of chronically sick.

But although the Poor Law doctors were most directly in contact with the mass of medical suffering, they were least able to protest about their conditions. If they were to advance themselves beyond these low standards of medicine, they had best avoid a quarrel. In the meantime they had to accept that they were inferior doctors for the inferior classes. The rod was, quite literally, shaken over nurses who spoke up for their patients. So the unvisited, unwanted patients were lumped together in stark, unadorned, unhygienic buildings, separated from their lifelong companions, lacking all rights and branded as 'idle' into the bargain. They were served cheap medicines and unhealthy food by staff who were as ill as the patients, leading what a contemporary visitor called 'a life that would be like that of a vegetable were it not that they preserve the doubtful privilege of sensibility to pain and mental misery'.

By the middle of the nineteenth century the two hospital services stood side by side: for the lucky and selected few in London and the big cities, splendid voluntary or teaching hospitals, provided, of course, their illness suited the doctor's interests; but the workhouse infirmaries, the real hospitals, and the Poor Law officers, who were the first salaried public-health doctors, were ignored as long as their burden on the taxpayer was kept to an absolute minimum.

Hospital reform

Late Victorian England saw a flurry of hospital reform, building and improvement. The sheer pressure of medical need apparent in cities thrown up more like standing camps than planned towns, the daily injuries to health inflicted by the factory system and the growing numbers of orphans, widows, deserted wives and old people who were quite without the traditional support from their relatives and the sheer speed at which the cities grew, all combined to demand more organised medical care quite beyond the abilities of the private medical sector. Systematic investigation of the exact state of the poor, pioneered by Booth and Rowntree, revealed the grim arithmetic of suffering which penetrated the ignorant self-satisfaction of the Victorian middle class. And the findings of the pioneer social investigators became a flood as they were joined by various well-intentioned laymen who made it their business to find out and improve the real conditions of the sick and poor.

War, as always, provided its macabre criticism of medicine: Florence Nightingale, who witnessed at first hand the collapse at Sebastopol in the Crimean War, proposed an almost military reform of nursing; and from the sick bed to which she retired periodically when unable to get her way and assisted by the male secretaries who were her clerical servants, she set about the reorganisation of everything from nursing education to hospital architecture, dispensing especially telling criticism of the sanitary arrangements within wards. The successive outbreaks of infectious fevers – the urban epidemics – especially the water-borne dysentry carried by the cholera vibrio which had the democratic tendency to afflict all classes equally, spurred the rapid building of large isolation hospitals as well as the better-known reforms of water supply, public drainage and sewerage, and slum housing pushed through by Sir John Simon in London, Percival and Ferrier in Manchester and Howard in Liverpool. Indeed, the separation of domestic water supply from sanitary drainage has proved a more lasting achievement of the Victorian middle class than their conquest of India. But it is the patients and the Poor Law doctors themselves who probably did most to dent the complacency of Parliament and the meanness of the Guardians, who, though aroused periodically by the writings of Dickens or the reports of Chadwick, equally forgot periodically, especially when finance rather than sympathy was demanded. The poor, especially the Northern textile workers who flatly refused to be punished by imprisonment in the workhouse during the regular trade depressions, had always hated the Bastilles. In Bradford in 1837 and Dewsbury and Todmorden in 1838, town-wide risings greeted the new Poor Law. And in the industrial areas workers' protests were abetted by the overseers, vestrymen and even magistrates themselves who, on principle, disliked any central direction. Although the political demands of working-class radical bodies did not seem to raise the problem of their sick fellows, the growing organised strength and impatience of workers lent urgency to efforts at reform. But Harney, the Chartist leader, could certainly have been speaking of the workhouse sick when he said: 'By Heavens, the patience – or rather suicidal apathy – of the masses is wonderful and pitiable.'

Workhouse doctors

Workhouse doctors, their status enhanced by the 1858 Act which put medical qualification and registration on a respectable footing, felt emboldened to take a stand against their exploitation by the Boards of Guardians and bullying by the masters, and to speak up for their abused patients. In 1866 Dr Rogers formed the Poor Law Medical Officers' Association and the *Lancet* lent its support to a national campaign for better treatment of sick paupers in the workhouse with its investigation and exposure of the state of the sick-wards in a number of London workhouses in 1865. With even more courage, nurses joined the protest about the neglect. Joan Bateman complained about the Paddington workhouse and Matilda Beeton went further in showing how the officials in Rotherhithe had deliberately, and easily, deceived the inspectors. The masters could sneer at ladies like Mrs Twining of the Workhouse Visiting Society, with their 'many imaginary grievances' and who 'sometimes go to the length of bestowing unmerited tea or even indigestible lozenges and Puseyite tracts upon our protegees'.[5]

They could not laugh off so easily the *Lancet*'s 'soberly sensational' findings and uncompromising conclusions:

> Patch up the present system as we may, it will still continue to be a scandal and a reproach. . . . The State hospitals are in the workhouse wards. They are closed against observation, they pay no heed to public opinion, they pay no toll to science. They are under the government of men profoundly ignorant of hospital rules.[6]

Prompted by fear of working-class wrath, by feeling for the poor's suffering, and the committed rationalism of a new breed of doctors, improvements were made: 'If a pauper cannot but envy us, it is desirable that he should hate us as little as possible', hoped a worried contributor to the *Saturday Review* in 1869.

Quite how far medical standards had risen by the end of the nineteenth century is hard to gauge. The authorities were less hostile to public-health measures and were beginning to see state provision of basic health needs as a necessary evil, not out of any great compassion, but in the over-all interests of effective production, competition and warfare. The charitable bodies, having themselves discovered the sheer weight of suffering, were despairing of remedying it themselves by stern advice and thin gruel alone. (Canon Samuel Barnett, a founder of the Charity Organisation Society and who broke with it in 1895, described his colleagues as 'clothing themselves in the dirty rags of their own self-righteousness'.) As the extent of poverty (a third of all Londoners were under Booth's poverty line in the 1890s) was documented in irrefutable detail, the sheer want could no longer be dismissed as unrepresentative or attributed to a deliberate unwillingness to work. But awareness and charitable endeavour over the poverty of their employees did not alter the harshness of the factory system one little bit. And in the last analysis it was the low wages, long hours and unsafe working conditions, made worse by the overcrowded housing and poor diet, which was the fundamental cause of much ill health.

The hospital service was clearly improving, especially in the London voluntary hospitals, where antisepsis transformed the possibilities of surgery. The traditional and well-justified fear of hospitals was now tempered with a respect for the new scientific knowledge possessed somewhere within their portals. Hospitals were more than a last resort. Evidence of their new esteem was the opening of wards to take fee-paying middle-class customers. They were elaborately screened (with thick canopies) from the eyes of their social inferiors, but the British Medical Association still thought that: 'It is at present doubtful if the curtained compartments of the large wards will ever be popular as it is evident there can be little real privacy under such an arrangement.' Great specialisation within medicine, as well as more commercial considerations, led to the establishment of a flush of special hospitals to which it was hoped patients might find their way direct. The bigger hospitals provided out-patient facilities at which the poor queued for treatment. There were also dispensing clinics for those who could not afford their own practitioner, although treatment was inevitably inadequate and incomplete. One patient remembers that 'there were rows and rows of forms and you would gradually shift up, shift up, till eventually, after a long wait, it was your turn and then you went in. The doctor of course would only spend a minute or so with each one as he had so many to deal with.'

General practitioners

General practitioners dispensed their medicine on the same basis as any other retail trade, setting fees the market could hold and were in direct competition with each other. In a rich district a doctor lived in style and dressed the part, with silk top hat, gold-headed cane and carriage. Practices with an established clientele were bought and sold between doctors, for wealthy patients, especially when chronically ill, were business assets. A hypochondriac pinioned to illness but successful in commerce was especially prized. But many doctors were very poor and those in working-class areas worked very much harder for small financial return. Often young doctors without social standing or wealthy backers were exploited by the doctor who owned the practice or by the paternalistic employers or charities who retained their services. Even then medical practitioners were not summoned lightly and illness was left until it proved serious; if you called him every time you were sick he would never be off your doorstep and you would never be out of debt (to the neighbours, that is, not to the doctor, who would expect immediate payment). Also, relatively few of the advances in medical science yet had direct application in general practice.

Recalling growing up in the Salford slums, Robert Roberts remembers the doctor as a jovial but ineffectual figure, a well-respected joke among people who knew only too well the limitations of the medicine he dispensed.[7] Minor ailments were accepted and many major ones doused with patent medicines and pain-killing draughts of opium-based cordials. A seamstress in Bethnal Green recalls her dying mother, exhausted with work, want and child-bearing:

> About the time I was nine years old, my mother used to be very poorly, and an old doctor advised her to take a little spirits. She was so often without money, and so often in want of a little drop of spirits, that I got into the habit of saving up all the pennies I could running errands or minding babies, and when my mother had one of her poorly turns I would spend my money and bring her the medicine I believed it to be. How little I knew what I was doing.[8]

Her doctor and her daughter had addicted her to gin, when she really needed medicine.

Dr Jolley, a delightfully cantankerous G. P. in Hackney, a 'three-penny doctor' and proud of it, was famous for his absence of bedside manner and his advice on nutritious foods and clean air; he organised a char-à-banc to take his patients to the seaside, even though it kept breaking down. Some elementary health education was carried out in emphatic style; Robert Roberts remembers:

> one local doctor whenever he was called upon our humbler neighbours with stomach troubles would demand the family frying

pan, then go outside and smash it against a wall; a gesture which compelled the housewife to borrow another one from next door until she could afford to buy another. She made no protest at the act; a doctor was a demi-god.[9]

In the coal-mining areas of the North, where private practice was never workable, the 'club' system, an important antecedent to the N. H. S. and an influence on Bevan, flourished. Here working men banded together to arrange the hiring of a doctor and sometimes the building of his premises or a cottage hospital by a levy on wages; they had therefore an organised say in the kind of medicine they received. This arrangement had elements of workers' local initiative and even of control which have subsequently been surrendered. But the quality of care under the club system was limited by the difficulty of gaining access to specialist opinion; a referral usually meant a trek to London with cash and cap in hand. Dr Danny Abse recalls being asked by a Welsh miner, 'You from Harley Street, are you?', when he attempted to use a stethoscope as late as the 1930s.[10]

But far from welcoming the steady expansion of hospital in-patient and clinic care, general practitioners resented it violently. It took their business away, patients' preference for the specialist elite rubbed them in the face of their professional inferiority, and they had genuine objections to the standard of care dispensed. Reform of the 'abuses' of free hospital care became a burning issue; the G. P.s disliked the clinics because they were providing more and more medical care to people who they felt ought to pay (although they would have disliked the hospitals still more had they charged). They wanted consultants to be genuine specialists and to accept patients only by referral. There was talk of gentlemen with pony carriages and private incomes spotted in hospital queues and of the sick journeying from hospital to hospital. One medical journal wrote:

> The whole country is a rickyard of hospitals and incendiaries in the shape of dissatisfied general practitioners who are carrying blazing torches in all directions . . . the weak place is the outpatient department . . . the number of cases that a 'physician' – save the mark! will see, examine and treat in an hour is incredible, and absolutely destructive of professional honesty. The plain truth is that some outpatient physicians do not care one straw for their outpatient work except in as far as it is a stepping stone to a permanent hospital appointment.[11]

The Association of General Practitioners was formed with the aim of confining consultants to consultation in the strict sense: 'The whole struggle between the general practitioner and the consultant is one of bread', wrote Dr. Rentoul a militant G. P. Financial self-interest divided the profession, put hospital and community medicine at loggerheads and ruled out free medicine even though the more far-sighted practitioners, especially those in most direct contact with the mass of the poor, could see the medical need for such a system. 'Sickness,' recommended the workhouse doctors in 1878, is 'one of the most prolific and pitiable sources of pauperism, ought to be placed on a footing quite apart from that of ordinary causes of want and dependence on the rates. It is cheap and wise to cure the sick poor with the greatest promptitude.'

The failure of Poor Law hospital reform

At the turn of the century, even though a brisk expansion of welfare services by the local authorities was in sight, the public provision of medicine was still third class and treatment of those rejected by the teaching hospitals and quite out of financial reach of private doctoring – those in most medical need – was haphazard and often cruel. The system of using pauper nurses under the incompetent supervision of the wives of the Masters persisted, because of its cheapness. Trained nurses willing to stomach the very long hours and cramped quarters and prepared to suffer the petty despotism of the Masters could not bear to see their skills wither from want of use or be lost on patients deemed by the system as chronic or incurable. As Beatrice Webb, the Fabian social reformer, pointed out about the Poor Law doctors, 'It breaks the spirit of a man who cares anything at all about his professional work to have to go on year after year merely pretending to deal with cases which have come to him only when destitution has set in.'[12] One nurse resigned because of the 'utter uselessness of nurses fighting for proper administration under un-trained management . . . we stand so often entirely unsupported'. So the scandals, or those that could not be covered up, persisted. In the workhouse at Christchurch 'a man, aged sixty, suffering from heart disease, was allowed to lie ill and groaning, cared for only by the inmates in the "old men's ward" of the workhouse, without proper food and attention, from Saturday night to Monday morning. He was then carried on the porter's back to the infirmary, where he died almost immediately'. In 1890, the sick-wards of the Bethnal Green workhouse were described by inquiring doctors as 'a crying and a notorious evil'. The workhouse medical officer described how he had to rely on the assistance of a friendly local G. P. to do the amputations which were still done 'underhanded', as it 'takes three men to get a leg off properly' – 590 sick paupers were crowded into wards for 495 patients, cared for by eleven nurses, only two of whom had had hospital training. On the national scale, the Webbs estimated in 1907 that the 10,000 patients in country workhouses were 'looked after' by only 654 nurses and 105 practitioners.[13]

Doctors remained low paid and their visits pretty token, so brief that they must have been confined to a cursory look at those new patients which the nurses could persuade them were worth examining. An inspector who studied the amount of time given to workhouse duties reported of one that 'frequently he has been only in the workhouse for a few minutes and that he had rarely been in the workhouse for half an hour'. A good part of that had to be spent passing the time of day with the Master and the Matron. Drugs were still paid for out of the doctor's own salary; this not only ruled out new or expensive drugs but even such staples as quinine and digitalis if the doctor was not to end up out of pocket. This system was described by one medical inspector as likely 'to cost the life of an inmate of a workhouse'. Another inspector reported in 1893 that, in the workhouse hospitals, 'operations were performed where private patients would undoubtedly have anaesthetics, whereas the paupers have to suffer without them'. It was as if the poor did not feel pain so much. In the words of Dicken's upper-class gentleman, Steerforth, 'Why there is a pretty wide separation between them and us. They are not to be expected to be as sensitive as we are . . . they have not such fine natures and they may be thankful that, like their coarse rough skins, they are not easily wounded'. The old principle of 'less eligibility' was firmly enforced, all poor relief, including that for the sick, had to be made less pleasant than even the most harsh means of living outside the workhouse, and that was dismal indeed. The excuse was, as always, the prevention of fraud and the encouragement of thrift. Poverty was still attributed to 'fraud, indolence and idleness', although anyone who bothered to find out would have seen that most of the poor were widows, children, old people, the sick and the disabled, whose state was certainly not their own fault. Relief, even if it had been much more adequate, would have done nothing to alter the causes and simply confirmed the poor in their passive state, reduced to imploring mercy and charity; and if these ideas were being modified in some areas, they were still alive and well in the minds of whose who had local control over the workhouses. They provided a lofty moral theory to justify the most small-minded cruelties whose real motive was the tight-fistedness of the Guardians rather than some elevated philosophy in the poor's best interest. To be a pauper was a legal status, deprived of even the right to vote, and humiliation was essential. It was most important, wrote Inspector Longley, that:

> the stamp of pauperism is plainly marked upon all relief given . . . the words 'Dispensary' and 'Infirmary' should never be used in forms, advertisements or addresses without the prefix 'Pauper' or 'Poor Law' or 'Workhouse', which should indeed appear as far as possible in every document supplied by Guardians to those relieved by them.[14]

Yet the shadow of the workhouse was always present in working-class life and because there was still no public provision by right for the old or the widowed, a family at one moment prosperous could be the next plummeted into the deliberate miseries of the workhouse. In 1895, the mother of Charlie Chaplin, that Dickens of the cinema, lost her actor husband and the grim sequence commenced:

> like sand in an hourglass, our finances ran out, and hard times again pursued us. . . . Instalment payments were behind, consequently Mother's sewing machine was taken away. . . . There was no alternative, she was burdened with two children, and in poor health; and so she decided that the three of us should enter the Lambeth workhouse . . . there we were made to separate, Mother going in one direction to the women's ward and we in another to the children's. How well I remember the poignant sadness of the first visiting day; the shock of seeing Mother entering the visiting room garbed in workhouse clothes. How forlorn and embarrassed she looked! In one week she had aged and grown thin.[15]

Investigation at last

To many of the Victorian middle class, welfare was immoral. The poor had only themselves to blame, to aid them in their distress was to encourage deliberately their idleness and undermine their resolve to triumph in the jungle of life. But the same gentlemen were also devoted to orderly planning and the greatest good for the greatest number of people, at minimum cost, of course. The two principles came more and more openly into conflict as the *laissez-faire* approach to welfare collapsed under the sheer weight of distress created by the factory system which had created the wealth of Britain. The 'defenders of the filth' could deny bitterly any connection whatsoever between dirt and disease, eulogise the open sewers and poisoned water as bracing and argue that dust had a positively beneficial effect on the lungs. But disease was a great leveller and no respecter of front parlours. It was easy for the more logical to argue that the state, acting in the over-all interest, needed new powers, including the power, as Simon put it, 'of doing away with that form of liberty to which some communities cling, the sacred liberty to poison unto death not only themselves but their neighbours'. In the same way, the deliberately low standards of the public hospitals, the reduction of the sick to the status of the poor and the sheer complexity of parallel sources of medical care were an affront to logic. The utter failure of the treatment of tuberculosis, the very poor diet and health standards revealed by education authorities' surveys and the shocking standard of physique found among army recruits made no economic or military sense. 'How can we get an efficient army out of the stunted, anaemic, demoralised denizens of the slum basements of our great cities?' asked Rosebery. Imperialism required 'national efficiency' and that required a break with old official Liberalism. Modern industrialists, too, saw the need for a fitter and more skilful labour force, even for collaboration with, rather than resistance to, union organisation.

In 1905 a Royal Commission set to work to report on the state of the Poor Law to resolve some of these conflicts. The stern defenders of the 1834 spirit argued that the sick should be clearly separated from the poor so as to better oppress the unemployed, who, now lacking even the excuse of illness, could be set to suffer at flint-crushing and cross-cut sawing. The radicals on the Commission wanted the breaking up of the Poor Law into various separate welfare schemes for the old, the unemployed and the unhealthy, administered by the local authorities and available free to all-comers. Beatrice Webb, a socialist with most authoritarian leanings, thought medicine itself ought to become compulsory: 'it suddenly flashed across my mind that what we had to do was to make medical inspection and medical treatment compulsory on all sick persons – to treat illness, in fact, as a public nuisance to be suppressed in the interests of the community'.[16]

Both sides agreed that moral deterrence alone was inadequate. Old-age pensions, which were introduced while the Commission sat, were commended, and it recommended that free hospital service should be rationalised and extended, and children with poverty-stricken or neglectful parents should be cared for publicly. Wards for the sick were to be finally separated from the workhouses and the ill diverted more often to the out-patient dispensaries. The emphasis was still on thrift and only very grudging aid, carefully tied to a record of past diligence. Sickness possessed moral overtones, the proposed system would be 'stimulating and educating those who, though sick, ought to have themselves made provision against sickness'. But the Commission was firmly divided over the extent of preventive welfare services for the poor, with the Webbs drafting a forceful minority report. And this split provided an official excuse for inaction. The workhouse hospitals were straddled on an impasse, unable to go back to the deterrent pattern but unable to move forward for a national preventative service. The Webb's blue-print for a State Medical Service though logically sound, encountered too many vested interests at once.

Such a service required the loss of the voluntary hospitals' jealously guarded independent status, and the organisation of the sick clubs and the doctors themselves by the public authorities was still anathema, although already glimpsed by some more visionary doctors as a possible solution. 'Book keeping, debt collection and bad debts', wrote Benjamin Moore, in praise of such a system, 'would have vanished like an evil dream and men would at last feel that he was an honoured member of a scientific profession, with time and interest to study the problems which he had chosen for his life's work instead of being as he now is, a small tradesman with a declining business.'[17]

National Insurance

It was less lofty motives which had led Lloyd George to introduce National Insurance. 'I hope our competition with Germany will not be in armaments alone', he boasted as he eyed the social benefits of the insurance scheme introduced by his arch-rivals. His 1911 Act established a compulsory contribution towards health which would provide the wage-earner with the right of free consultation with a general practitioner who prescribed free drugs, and entitlement to sickness benefit when absent from work through illness. 'The Panel' and 'The Stamp' were born; it is from 1911 that the phrase 'getting your cards' stems, referring to the form on which the employer's contribution was affixed. The scheme faced the formidable vested interests of the private health insurance companies with whom the skilled artisan had increasingly contributed, as well as the doctors who were initially fiercely opposed to the Bill, reacting, as is often the case, with something little short of hysteria when any changes are proposed to their own profession. In fact, it was a splendidly convenient scheme. It provided the appearance of an alternative to a national health service, but by collaborating with, rather than replacing, the insurance giants. It was a method of replacing the Poor Law with very modest Treasury expenditure.

Although new social service for the working class might appear, if you listened to the doctors, a massive act of generosity, it was in fact paid for by that class, administered by the insurance companies (under new names) and produced a very sharp increase in income for most doctors who worked with the panel scheme. They could now supplement their private fee-paying work with the government's *per capita* payment for treating panel patients. As the doctor's maid puts it daintily in Arnold Bennett's *Elsie and the Child*: 'You had two voices, one for "them" and their friends and the private patients and another for Joe and the tradesmen and panel patients.'

Like Bevan, Lloyd George made much of his battles with the profession during what he called 'the wrangle in the sickroom':

> I had two hours discussion with the medical men themselves the other day. I don't think there has been anything like it since the day when Daniel went into the lions' den. I was on the dissecting table for two hours but I can assure you that they treated me with the same courtesy as the lions treated my illustrious predecessor.

And the Welsh wizard was to encounter the persistent heckle of 'Taffy was a Welshman, Taffy was a thief' by serving girls sent by their mistresses, irate about the effect that licking the employers' 3d stamp per week would have on both their fair lips and their pockets. But it is clear that even he realised the conservative nature of the 1911 Bill as a substitute for a radical transformation of the Poor Law. He memoed a civil servant in 1911:

> Insurance [is a] necessary temporary expedient. At no distant date hope State will acknowledge full responsibility in the matter of

making provision for sickness, breakdown and unemployment. It really does so now, through Poor Law but the conditions under which this system has hitherto worked have been so harsh and humiliating that working class pride revolts at accepting so degrading and doubtful a boon.

The limitations

The Lloyd George scheme was so full of expectations and limitations that it leaked. Only wage-earners were eligible and venereal- and alcohol-related diseases were specifically excluded, so only about 30 per cent of the population benefited directly. It did not cover those whose general health was really bad, the wives and children of the poor and unemployed. There was no provision for hospitalisation, for which many workers continued to insure privately or by means of subscription to a voluntary hospital; nor was X-ray examination, physiotherapy or after-care nursing provided. Many drugs were excluded and there was no provision for dental care, artificial limbs, specialist eye-care or an optical service, although bad eyesight and poor teeth accounted for a large reserve of treatable illness which, undiagnosed, worsened and caused more serious illness. The administration of the service was carried out by the existing societies, who were required to operate democratically and on a non-profit basis but did neither. Rather than being replaced by the Act, the insurance companies became the administrative agents for it. Because hospital and specialist care was untouched by the scheme, they were pressed into ever-worsening financial straits. The approved societies had the option to refuse cases and, as insurance companies always will, protected their coffers by trying to eliminate known health risks.

The emphasis was still on a bare minimum coverage, the system aiming to minimise hardship during acute illness rather than forestall it, and the patient was told from all sides not of what he was entitled to but how he ought to be grateful. Cash benefit during illness was low, even allowing for the fact that it was meant only to cover the sick person and not dependants. Insurance rather than a national health service was renewed; the companies' collectors now had access to homes to which they could proceed to market services that the 1911 Act did not cover. Anyway, at the home, to collect the sickness benefit for an ill patient, the canvasser might, after expressing his sympathies in the sickroom, sell a burial policy in the kitchen; the government had given a great fillip to the underwriters.

Local action

Probably more important was the growing ability of local authorities to provide welfare services. School meals and medical inspection were begun, and revealed children stunted before they were ten, strangers to fresh milk and seeing meat but once a week. The Lambeth School Inspector had reported in 1903 that 'want of food, irregularity and unsuitability, taken together are the determining cause of degeneracy in children. The breakfasts that these children get are normally bread and tea, if they get it at all.' But 1900 and 1913 local-authority spending almost doubled. Here working-class radicals became more assertive, stating for the first time that free medicine and good health ought to be possessed by every citizen, by right and not out of administrative convenience or to provide sturdy cannon-fodder. In East London Sylvia Pankhurst turned her back on the campaign for the vote and the House of Commons, 'where courage evaporates like a bubble', and organised the working women and wives to arrange their own clinics, crèches and restaurants. The East London Federation of Suffragettes converted a pub to what must have been one of the first maternity centres and renamed it *The Mother's Arms*. From it a resident nurse ran a string of mother and baby clinics, dispensed cheap maternity foods and health, sex education and hygiene talks; and in the same part of London, George Lansbury and the Labour Councillors of Poplar were imprisoned in Brixton Gaol in 1921 rather than cut down on the local relief as the Tory-controlled London County Council was insisting.

Lansbury argued the socialist case for welfare: that those who had wealth ought to support those who did not. Why should working-class areas which bore the brunt of unemployment shoulder that burden themselves when middle-class residences, places with more wealth, did not have any unemployed to maintain? He bellowed his case from the basement cell of his gaol to the crowds who would march across from East London every night, and, conducted by a striking policeman, serenade the imprisoned councillors in their dungeons. Poplar council's refusal to make economies in the face of basic human need brought the support of the people of Bethnal Green, who voted to follow their lead, with Stepney and Battersea not far behind. 'Poplarism', i.e. local councils going on strike against national cuts, spread quickly. The government backed down and then introduced a Bill that equalised rate burdens, increased unemployment benefits and made them a nationally administered matter.

The patients, the poor and the unemployed were coming out of the shadows of gloom and guilt in which they had been consigned as firmly as in the workhouse. They were starting to ask for their rights. No wonder Beatrice Webb, the mistress of social reform from above, was horrified by 'the utter recklessness' of Lansbury. She wanted reform carried out by an all-powerful state for the national interest. But when the poor themselves said what they wanted, the demand for welfare from below infuriated her.

2

The coming of national health

By the First World War there was the beginnings of a public medical service, even if it was operated by private medical practitioners and the insurance companies. But it was strictly limited to the generally male wage-earners, access to a second opinion or hospital specialist treatment was uneven, still dependent on financial rather than medical circumstances. G. P.s still earned the bulk of their income from fees supplemented by part-time work for the health authorities. The voluntary hospitals' standards were improving steadily, although the attendance of the 'honorary' consultants who were supposed to run them was sporadic. Over half a million, mainly the aged and chronic sick, still languished in Poor Law beds, no less than 35,864 in general mixed workhouses as late as 1928. Relations between practitioner and hospital had improved, although there was still much scaremongering about G. P.s 'with rusty scalpels and distorted forceps running about crying out "Who can I try my skill on?"'. Unhappily the state scheme was still grafted on to a much older pattern of medical private enterprise, self-help, charity and Poor Law cruelty.

But the haphazard national distribution and the maze-like pattern of clubs, dispensaries, hospitals and private contracts resulted in a divided national hospital service and two very different standards of health care, which was proved but not solved by the First World War. Although some sort of state medical service was eventually provided on the front line, it differed widely according to the class of the injured, with officers, for example, still entitled to a Red Cross Grant to pay their servants' wages during convalescence in Harrogate or on the Riviera, while in the front line it was common for soldiers to die without encountering medical aid. Also, the civilian service suffered badly, with the tuberculosis rate in particular increasing sharply during the war.

The new dawn

Elaborate promises were made about the 'new dawn' at the end of the First World War. Lloyd George promised not only a 'land fit for heroes' and to 'hang the Kaiser' but also the implementation of the McLean Report on public health and the establishment of a Ministry of Health. Even the White Papers and Blue-books reflected the mood. The Interim Report of the Adult Education Committee said in 1918:

> No one can doubt that we are at a turning point in our national history. A new era has come upon us. We cannot stand still. We cannot return to our old ways, the old abuses, the old stupidities. As with our international relations so with the relations of classes and individuals inside our own nation, if they do not henceforth get better they must needs get worse, and that means moving towards an abyss.

And for two years trade boomed, wages held up at wartime levels, and a new confidence won at the work-place by the syndicalist and socialist trade unionists during the war seemed to press home its advantage. Lloyd George and the Coalition pledged 'all services relating to the care and treatment of the sick and infirm shall not be administered as part of the Poor Law but should be a part of the general health services of this country'. The Labour Party called for the reconstruction 'not of this or that piece of social machinery, but of society itself', calling for the state to assume responsibility for a minimum level of health with social services paid for by progressive taxation and administered by local authorities.

Old problems

By 1921 a massive slump sent unemployment soaring. By the end of 1921 there were nearly two million unemployed. The National Insurance dyke collapsed under the strain: how could a contributory scheme hold up when people were so seldom in work? The dole, money over and above the strict level paid in contributions, was only given in certain cases. In 1927, after the crushing of the General Strike, even the dole was withheld if the official suspected the applicant was 'not genuinely seeking work', even there was none to be found. Then, finally, a family means test was introduced. The new dawn had been brief, the old abuses and the old stupidities were back. For the disabled soldiers, too ill to work but without pensions, the old, whose meagre pension even with public assistance could not cover fuel and food for the week, for lads and lasses with no prospect of work and less food than their parents had known, the world of the rich on the radio and in the picture houses must have been painful to watch.

The 'hungry thirties'

The 'hungry thirties' started here, in the mid-1920s: hunger for basic human needs, for protein, for warm clothes, for dry homes, was already stunting physiques and dragging health standards downward. Whatever the quality of health provision, chronic poor diet among those out of work weakened their resistance to tuberculosis, made the common cold develop to epidemic proportions, produced sickly infants and dead babies in the labour bed. Mental depression was so common, it was not even diagnosed. Moral authorities contented themselves with complaining about the half-starved's curious desire for cheap palliatives like chocolate and football pools. The medical needs for life itself were the subject of a propaganda battle. The British Medical Association produced a specimen diet to be used as a basis for assessing the needs of the unemployed which proved embarrassingly to be rather lower than that which was provided by the Scottish prison authorities to their convicts. Even so it was estimated that one in five lived near or below that meagre margin. Wal Hannington, leader of the Unemployed Workers' Movement, protested that this controversy meant that:

the poor unemployed worker and his family looked on at this new capitalist game of treating human beings like so many test tubes. There was much talk of calories, alphabetical vitamins, proteins, carbohydrates, fats and grammes, which all sound like a foreign language to the ordinary unemployed worker whose family was having to exist on a diet composed chiefly of potatoes, bread, margarine, tea and condensed milk.[1]

The Ministry's evidence was clearly biased. They managed to deny 'widespread manifestation of impaired health which could be attri-

buted to insufficient nourishment' within miles of an area in the
Rhondda where Lady Williams's charitable food distribution programme had reduced maternal mortality by 75 per cent. Geographical
differences amplified class factors. In the old industrial areas in Wales
and the North-east, the entire population was without work and the
towns were turned to stone, while employed workers in the South
improved their standards of life despite the Depression and the
conditions of the rural poor probably stayed fairly constant. No one
could deny the relation between class and illness. To take the single
most fundamental index, the infant death rate, it was in 1935 only 42
per thousand live births in the Home Counties, 63 in Glamorgan, 76
in Durham, 77 in Scotland, 92 in Sunderland and 114 in Jarrow.
Medical examination was becoming more extensive and more
devastating in its findings. The results of the $2\frac{1}{2}$ million examinations
of young men completed in the last year of the First World War
showed that of every nine men, only three were fit and healthy and
'two were on a definitely infirm plane of health and strength, whether
from some disability or failure in development; three were incapable
of undergoing more than a very moderate degree of physical exertion,
and could almost (in view of their age) be described as physical
wrecks; and the remaining man was a chronic invalid with a
precarious hold on life'.[2]

Nine per cent of schoolchildren's eyes were suffering defects, dental
standards were appalling, a full set of teeth being a rarity in working-
class mouths. People only saw a dentist if pain was intolerable and
then for extractions only. Dr McGonigle found that 83 per cent of
children examined in County Durham rickety and although the
official figure was as low as 1.2 per cent McGonigle's higher figure
was supported by a 1937 survey which found only 12 per cent of 1638
children free from rickets with two-thirds showing serious signs of
disease. Another survey found alternations in pelvic bones of
mothers due to diet deficiency in 40 per cent of women attending the
antenatal centre. Midwives, although popular because closer to the
real lives of poor mothers, lacked rudimentary facilities, knew little
about antisepsis and were often paid in kind. The official inquiry into
the rising maternal death rate estimated half the deaths in pregnancy
were directly preventable. The Workers' Birth Control Group
campaigned in the Labour Party for extension of maternity benefits
with the slogan, 'It's four times as dangerous to bear a child as to go
down a mine'. Against such a stark background, the very piecemeal
improvements in hospital care, with the Poor Law hospitals finally

brought under the local authorities in 1929 and the growing integration of the voluntary hospitals, as of little avail as long as general practice remained purely palliative, G. P.s operating as private entrepreneurs and still in informal competition with the hospitals. Whooping cough, for example, for which a vaccine existed, still claimed over 2000 deaths in the worst years because there was no machinery for mass immunisation; and for many, death took place remorselessly, still woefully out of touch with the medical and surgical advances that existed in the best centres.

Aneurin Bevan

It was in this gaunt world that Aneurin Bevan, the architect of the National Health Service, grew up. He shaped his political ideas against the outline of the 'hungry thirties', in which the hideous townships, broken families and the silent steelworks mocked the claims of capitalist economics. He saw Parliament as 'a public mourner for private economic crimes' and the Tories as a political party whose task was 'to beguile democracy into voting wealth back to power each election'. He knew at first hand the human suffering caused by a welfare system based on organised stinginess, where the price of lives were merely an item in the cost of things and there were no aims that could not be accounted for on a balance-sheet. The texture of his life shaped all his ideas in class form. The question was: where does power lie, and how can it be obtained by the workers?

He knew, too, the medical traditions of the South Wales miners whose lungs, eyes and limbs suffered in the pits, and who formed working men's clubs to choose and supervise their own doctors in hospitals owned by the community. He came from a world where collective action to organise society and active trade-union involvement in health was assumed. His father, who died in his arms of pneumoconiosis, was a founder member of the Tredegar Working Men's Medical Aid Society. Bevan saw health as a field in which individual commercialism ran counter to most social values. To him it was illogical as well as unfair to prevent illness by private effort, or to make access to medical care dependent on ability to pay. Illness was above all a field in which 'poverty should not be a disability' and, equally important, 'wealth not an advantage'. He wrote that 'A free health service is a triumphant example of the superiority of collective action and public initiative applied to a segment of society where commercial principles are seen at their worst.' Those who argued that a free service rather than a fee service would invite abuse were forejudging the issue. What was more likely was an initial rush of demand deriving from past neglect. In the future, Bevan shrewdly predicted, abuse was much more likely to arise where private commercial interests overlapped with the national service. His vision was not administrative, it went beyond mere security to serenity and the sheer pleasure of enjoyed good health. 'What is this world,' he liked to say, 'if full of care, we have no time to stand and stare?.'

The Second World War

The need for reform was very widely accepted, although the doctors and Lord Beveridge were more concerned with the efficiency of the system than the desires of the people it served. The Second World War, with bombing placing, for the first time, most emergency medical pressure away from the front line and in the industrial centres, highlighted the unevenness of hospital standards and the rudimentary state of the pathology, blood-transfusion and ambu-lance services. Dispersed specialists insisted on the upgrading of the standards and services they discovered in hospitals they would never otherwise have visited. Doctors drafted into the army found that the salaried service, far from destroying their professional identity, enhanced their status and for most doctors their standard of living. A national survey of hospitals, a medical Domesday Book, was at last carried out. The Emergency Medical Service accustomed all those in the health service to a degree of centralisation, state control and obedience which the war effort as a whole demanded.

Even before the war specialist opinion had been in favour of an extension of the Health Insurance provisions and the P. E. P. Report in 1937 had found 'that a substantial part of the annual cost of ill health is due to delay in treatment. This delay is largely accounted for by the fact that doctors and dental fees are an expense people are loth to incur.' Churchill himself acknowledged 'that disease must be attacked in the same way that a fire engine will give its full assistance to the humble cottage as readily as it will give it to the most important mansion'. The Coalition government had already drawn up welfare plans which drew on the rationalisations and changes in gear the war footing had permitted and which could be offered as a genuine reason for fighting the war with gusto. Uncharitable as it might seem, the oldest argument for a national health service, put by Francis Bacon, i.e. that 'nothing forwards the conclusion of business so much as good health', was telling yet again.

The 1945 election result, an unexpected and overwhelming triumph for Labour, showed that the people who had fought and suffered the war were ungrateful to the Tory who had directed it, and were in a radical mood. Laski had ended the Labour Party's annual conference with a call for a clear choice 'between private enterprise now expressed as monopoly capitalism, and socialism that realises that the new age is born and that only through the establishment of a Socialist Commonwealth can we realise the purposes for which we have been fighting this war'. At the same conference a certain Denis Healey, a skittish young major, defied military protocol by mounting the platform in uniform and announcing: 'The upper classes in every country are selfish, depraved, dissolute, and decadent'.

Another new dawn

Bonfires were lit in the street and, as Michael Foot has put it, 'no socialist who saw it will forget the blissful dawn of July 1945'. The People's War had, it seemed, led to a People's Peace. The defeats and humiliations that followed the First World War, the General Strike, the 1931 betrayal, would be repaid. Instead, the Tories and their system swallowed their pride and lived to fight another day. Never has there been a more evident demonstration of Bevan's own favourite maxim: 'We are hard outside and soft within, the Tories are soft outside but hard within.' Even the National Health Service Bevan established was compromised. Apparently the high point of the reform, it has proved an excellent example of how the established forces can, in time, turn those reforms to their own advantage.

The Act was bold in outline; a national health service entirely free at the time of use, financed out of general taxation and able to organise preventative medicine, research and para-medical aids on a national basis. It entailed the taking of the voluntary hospitals into public ownership, close, in Tory eyes, to rapine. The Bevan plan aimed at an invigoration of general practice by the establishment of health centres where groups of doctors could work in liaison with each other's special skills and experience and with nurses and social-work staff.

Bevan himself was a politician apparently well prepared to deal with the conservative pressures which were bound to press upon his ministerial head. He was notorious for incurring Prime Minister

Attlee's wrath by eschewing the formal dress which he regarded as the livery of the ruling class. He had rejected the well-upholstered leather chair of the previous Minister of Health, saying sweetly, 'This won't do. It drains all the blood from my head and explains a lot about my predecessors.' These are details, but are an indication that he anticipated the outbreak of near-hysteria by doctors so skilfully orchestrated by Charles Hill of the British Medical Association who had endeared himself to the listening public as the wartime Radio Doctor with smooth-spoken concern for the regularity of their bowel motions facing the undeniably constipating effects of tinned snoek and powdered egg. And yet a bargain was struck rather than a victory won. Medical care changed a gear but in so doing transposed rather than resolved the conflicts within it.

The appointed day

Within a year of its inception 41,200,000 people were covered by the National Health Service. 'Workman's Insurance' had gone national, paupers were now citizens, what had been grudgingly given as assistance was there as of right. The sight of people trying on spectacles like gloves in their local Woolworths, the clatter of ill-fitting dentures and the hateful sight of nurses and sisters selling flags and collecting money for their hospitals were abolished. In the first year 187,000,000 prescriptions were written out by over 18,000 general practitioners, 8,500,000 dental patients treated and 5,250,000 pairs of glasses prescribed. 'I shudder to think', speculated Bevan, 'of the ceaseless cascade of medicine which is pouring down British throats at the present time.' Churchill did not miss the chance to suggest Bevan ought to be among the first to seek free psychiatric advice. But the degree of change was more in appearance than in reality.

Firstly, the grand aims of the plans were circumscribed by the extremely weak economic position; by 1948 it is estimated that without the direct aid through the Marshall Plan, rations of butter, sugar, cheese and bacon would have had to be cut by one-third, cotton goods would have virtually disappeared from the home market, timber shortages would have reduced the housing pro-gramme from about 200,000 new buildings a year to about 50,000, and shortages of other raw materials would have led to 1,500,000 unemployed.[3] It would take exceptional determination to press ahead with the building of new health centres when homes themselves were in question. Already the over-all economic situation shaped the medical options. And although Bevan had a keen appreciation of the limitations of reforms within the existing social framework, he was unable and politically unwilling to challenge them. Instead he sought to exact the most skilful compromise within the existing balance of power by gaining the acceptance of the most influential part of the medical world, the consultants and the Royal Colleges, against their G. P. colleagues by 'choking their mouths with gold'. As a medical historian of the transaction, Vincent Navarro, put it: 'As the Labour Government had done in other sectors of nationalised industry, it bought the collaboration of owners and managers of skills and property by crossing their palms with gold. And the amount of gold depended on their class as professional position within British society and within the NHS specifically.' For such was the generosity of the settlement that, as Brian Abel-Smith, the historian of British hospitals, said, 'The most aristocratic and reactionary bodies had found it easiest to come to terms with "socialism".' One B. M. A. member recalled: 'We assembled at that first meeting expecting that our beautiful profession was to be hung, drawn and quartered. Instead we were reprieved . . . on one point after another – control by local authorities, the free choice of patient and doctor, clinical freedom – the Minister had accepted what we were demanding before we had the opportunity of asking for it.' The workers and the soldiers had wanted a new deal and expected Bevan, of all people, to get one. But they had gone back to work and, in the long and winding corridors of power, the professionals had recovered the initiative.

The hospitals

The nationalisation of the hospitals was potentially the most emotive issue, given the traditional tenacity with which the voluntary hospitals had fought for existence. But these hospitals were also bankrupt and their consultants were weary of giving their services on a purely honorary basis. Their absolute medical authority no longer compensated for their non-existent salary. And given the growing cost of medical equipment, only the state, the war had demonstrated, was able to supply finance which could bring the outlying hospitals up to modern standards. When a stethoscope and a top hat to put it in were the only essential investments, a physician could ply his trade and take his chances in the flurry of competition for private practice in London. But that kind of medicine was eclipsed. More and more consultants required resources and ancillory technical staff and equipment which could only be provided in a hospital setting. It was in their interest to have a salaried post in a well-run hospital even if it was outside the traditional centres, especially if an access route to private work remained open. Lord Moran, or 'Champagne Charlie' as he was known among the G. P.s in honour of his reported love of late-night carousels with the new Minister, recalls a conversation he had with Bevan on this subject:

> *Bevan*   I find the efficiency of the hospitals varies enormously. How can that be put right?
> *Moran*   You will only get one standard of excellence when every hospital has a first rate consultant staff. At present the consultants are all crowded together in the large centres of population. You've got to decentralise them.
> *Bevan*   That's all very well, but how are you going to get a man to leave his teaching hospital and go into the periphery? [He grinned.] You wouldn't like it if I began to direct labour.
> *Moran*   Oh, they'll go along if they get an interesting job and if their financial future is secured by a proper salary.
> *Bevan* [after a long pause]   Only the State could pay those salaries. This would mean the nationalisation of hospitals.[4]

This approach conflicted with the interests of local-government and municipal Labour Party men like Herbert Morrison and with the right wing of the Labour Cabinet, like Dalton, who counselled 'to proceed by stages, spread over years, and not by one bold stroke'. Bevan's stroke was to set up appointed Regional Hospital Boards; this in effect merged the existing interests who had run the voluntary and the municipal hospitals with a direct helping of doctors. Although obliged to consult, the Ministry had absolute power, but in practice he was to allow the consultants the run of the hospitals. At his first meeting with the doctors he had impressed with his urbanity, although the snobbery of the B. M. A. negotiators was not hard to dent. 'We were quite surprised,' said Dr Cockshut, 'to discover he talked English.'[5] In an after-dinner speech, Bevan announced: 'I want for the miners, the railwaymen, the engineers, a far greater share in the management of their work and the policies that govern it, and I say no less for the doctors.' But what he was allowing was no more workers' control than control of mines by, say, the lift operators would be. In reality it was professional self-rule, a point made in the

House by Dr Stephen Taylor from the Labour benches, who feared by the attempt to combine 'industrial democracy' with 'general democracy' there was 'a danger that we may impose on ourselves a medical dictatorship, and a very bad thing that would be'. The consultants ruled the new health service and although they are by no means the ignoble predators popular in socialist mythology, they were bound to shape the health service, above all the new generations of doctors, in their own mould.

The teaching hospitals remained exempt from the new pattern of hospital government, driving a coach and six through the national system. The top doctors gained part-time sessional payment for their self-supervised sessions, to be augmented by 'merit awards' and the right to private practice, carried on, for their convenience, in the N. H. S. hospitals. The secretly-awarded merit awards were described at the time as designed 'to ensure a practical and imaginative way of securing a reasonable differentiation of income and providing relatively high earnings for the significant minority' but might be more bluntly described as a unique system of private bribery administered with public money in utter secrecy.

The tri-partite system

The administration of the general practitioner service, the pharmaceutical service, the dental service and the ophthalmic service was to be undertaken by new bodies called Executive Councils. Here the private insurance companies were the losers but were poorly organised in the health sector and sufficiently profitable elsewhere to scarcely resist. Health centres provided by the local authorities were to be the main feature of the primary care service. Doctors were to be paid by a mixture of capitation fee, a per-head fee according to the size of their list, and salary. The sale of 'goodwill' of a practice was halted, although a sum of £66 million was allocated to compensate practitioners for the loss of that right. The remaining local services, including child care, health visiting, home nursing and the ambulance service, were the responsibility of the local authority and the range of services was extended and made compulsory rather than just optional. In general within the hospital the role of the G. P. contracted and that of the consultant correspondingly enlarged. General-practice lists increased very rapidly but the character and resources of the family doctor's medicine hardly altered. Private practice as a whole declined as soon as it became clear that the clinical expertise of Harley Street was now freely available and the pickings of what private work survived was reserved for the hospital-based consultant. Rather than the unseemly fighting over the prosperous patient, doctors from now on would be more ready to complain about having their colleagues' 'problem patients' foisted upon them. After the initial noisy resistance, G. P.s also fell into line. Their *per capita* payment proved an acceptable half-way house between the logical but politically unacceptable salaried system favoured by the Left and the fee-for-service basis the dental practitioners successfully insisted upon.

In hindsight, general practice and public health were neglected grievously, cast out into the fields of worthy neglect as hospital medicine flourished. But at the time G. P.s seemed fairly satisfied at the new financial arrangements; and the birth of the N. H. S. must have seemed just one aspect of the beginning of a new era of peace, prosperity and guaranteed welfare for all. All the reforms of the early post-war years were underwritten by full employment, constantly rising living standards, the new world alliance with the United States. The new backdrop of affluence cast a rosy hue over all post-war reforms. The glow was assumed to be endless. We look back in a different light: the boom that buoyed up the National Health Service has subsided; the full employment and comprehensive welfare services planned by Beveridge are already in the past; the 'social-democratic assumptions' are no longer taken for granted: we face head-on the conflicts – over N. H. S. financing, primary care, private practice, the drug industry, health and safety at work – which Bevan dodged so eloquently.

The foundation of the N. H. S., hallowed in Labour Party mythology as the decisive battle in a terrible and hard-fought war for a new order, seems something altogether more modest, in essential continuity with pre-war liberal thinking and wartime practice. There is little that is genuinely new, much that attained its radical appearance from the optimisim of the times. David Stark-Murray of the Socialist Medical Association, a man closely involved with the foundation of the N. H. S., notes laconically: 'In the atmosphere of 1946 when people were ready for great new moves, it seems strange that Bevan . . . did not see and did not grasp the opportunity to break with the past.'[6]

3

The National Health Service: thirty years on

Thirty years after Bevan founded it with such clamour, the National Health Service has become a national institution as British as the Battle of Britain or Wimbledon. Like the Monarchy, it is an institution at the same time beyond fundamental criticism and the subject of interminable complaint. It has become the single largest employer in the country and nearly three-quarters of its £5000 million turnover is spent on the wages of its 800,000 employees, from the eminent consultant on merit award to the night domestic staff on their pittances. It is the tenth biggest single employing unit in the world. Since its foundation in 1948 it has increased its staff by 75 per cent, hospital admissions have risen by over 80 per cent, new out-patient appointments by a third, bottles of blood issued rose four times, and ambulance journeys increased threefold. General practitioners signed 45 per cent more prescriptions in 1975 than in the first year of the service. Over a million people make contact with the N. H. S. every day.

Between 1949 and 1975, the expectation of life at birth rose from 66.3 years to 69.1 years for a man and from 71 to 75.3 years for a woman. The death rate of newly born children was cut by a half and the number of mothers who died in child-birth fell to a fraction of its former level. Diseases like tuberculosis shrunk in menace from the status of an everyday killer to a clinical rarity, epidemics of polio and diphtheria were almost forgotten, the incidence of serious infectious illness has fallen sharply. Only as recently as 1941, 2400 children had perished from diphtheria. Medical planning, fair shares, the idea that the well ought to provide for those afflicted with sickness, all were accepted, even if it had taken a world war to do it.

But look again. Our record on infant mortality has indisputably improved, but by no means as fast as other Western European countries. Britain now lies twelfth in the European league table and one of the most comprehensive medical investigations ever carried out, the Court Report, which found that 'Infant mortality is a holocaust equal to all the deaths of the succeeding 24 years of life', concluded that 'children still die in our lifetimes of nineteenth century reasons'. People live longer, but the rate of improvement is now much slower than earlier in the century. And what kind of life do the old, approaching death, enjoy? Do they live or just survive? Is the increased volume of prescriptions, the antibiotics for virus infections which they do not cure, and tranquillisers for worries they do not solve, doing more good to the patient or the company that manufactures them? What kind of medicine do the N. H. S. doctors practise and is it really what the patients want? How much does our enthusiasm for the principles of the N. H. S. overshadow our candour about its faults? How much improvement in the health statistics can doctors honestly take credit for?

These questions are hard to answer with confidence. Statistics, even where they exist, and the N. H. S. has been notoriously bad at evaluating its own performance, are only averages of arbitrary agglomerates. As one of the most penetrating investigators of the real conditions of the N. H. S., Dr A. H. Baker, noted in 1972, 'I am concerned at the very considerable gap between the generally accepted policies and the reality of the service as patients find it.' Health is about such intangible things as dignity, suffering and confidence, and it is here that a service which is not based on commercial considerations gives its most important but most intangible value. To pay tribute to the most inspiring aims of Bevan, the first requirement is honesty; and to be honest, and to be realistic about what still needs to be done, we must be much less grandiose in our claims than is customary with so many of the politicians who water Bevan's grave with their crocodile tears.

Early days

What can be said with certainty about the early days of the N. H. S. is that proper specialist care, and with it the new technical equipment for X-ray and pathology laboratory investigation, arrived for the first time in areas of the country which had depended hitherto on the shaky skills and apparatus of the local practitioner. The available medical skill no longer aligned in the big cities and around the teaching hospitals in the magnetic field of the potential paying customer. Instead central taxation provided specialists with a living more attractive than the fee rat-race, as well as the equipment needed to undertake modern medical practice. Local authorities also set about the provision of ambulance services, home helps, district nurses and day centres as an accepted part of their work rather than an optional extra.

Here the most immediate gain was for surgical patients, especially married women who had been nursing known ailments because of the difficulty of getting the services of consultant surgeons until their condition became acute. A huge body of silently endured discomforts – fallen wombs, stress incontinence, heavy periods, the involuntary passing of water in old women and the reverse in men – was tackled. Like the pent-up demand for dentures and spectacles, this demonstrated not the patient's greed but the extent of untreated illness; but for the medical patients their health improved because of better living standards and the individual researchers in the laboratories rather than through a better service from their general practitioners.

At the beginning of the century, arsenic for syphilis, alkalis for urinary infection and aspirin for fever were the most effective drugs, but the biochemical breakthrough during the Second World War altered in a fundamental way the terms on which doctors faced serious illness. The sulphonamides were the first in an army of antibiotics which transformed treatment and mortality from infectious illness and began to make irrelevant the sanatoria and isolation hospitals of the past. Synthetic substitutes for body hormones enabled the replacement treatment of diabetes and thyroid diseases and prepared the ground for the Pill. Anaesthesia improved greatly in safety with muscle relaxants and improved breathing and resuscitation equipment making surgery safer, and severe but temporary shock possible to deal with. Blood-matching and transfusion services had been greatly improved by the prodding of war. But the standards and conditions of general practice were altered in no fundamental way; in some cases the work load increased and the medical basis remained the diagnostic snap judgement rather than scientific investigation. And many of the general social assumptions upon which the N. H. S. rested have proved unreliable.

The end of poverty?

Looking back to the 1950s, on the faces of officialdom concerned with all aspects of welfare is an unstated smugness: the conviction that poverty was a thing of the past, that the affluent society had come to stay, that we had never had it so good and were going to have it even better in the future. Looking back, it seems like a willed self-deception, even though it was based on real, if not permanent changes in British society. One economist estimates that 'the system as a whole has never grown so fast for so long as since the war – twice as fast again between 1950 and 1964 as between 1913 and 1950, and nearly half as fast again as during the generation before that'.[1] Antony Crosland, the leading theorist of the Labour Party, was convinced that this change was permanent: 'Capitalism,' he wrote, 'has been reformed almost out of recognition. Despite occasional minor recessions and balance-of-payments crises, full employment and at least a tolerable level of stability are likely to be maintained.'[2]

The poverty of the 1930s had been caused by lack of work; post-war full employment reversed this, the associated rise in wage rates protected it and such wartime welfare measures as food subsidies and family allowances smoothed out hardship. The only remaining problem was to locate pockets of suffering and bring them up to par; there was no problem which could not be solved by an allowance or a prescription. In health Beveridge's assumption that spending would tend to fall as ill-health was identified, isolated and treated was widely accepted. Deceived by the external appearance of affluence, social theory tended to attribute any lingering misfortune to poor adjustment, absent fathers or problem families, where conceptions wrenched from their psychoanalytic origins were projected as explanations of personal or family inadequacies.

Looking backwards, the most striking factor in official thinking is ignorance. As the authors of a very detailed study of the poor in Nottingham observe:

> Only a decade later, we now know that throughout the fifties the numbers of people in poverty could already be counted in millions and were growing not shrinking; that the distribution of national wealth was becoming less, not more, equitable; that the much vaunted equalities of opportunity were to a great extent paper promises rarely carried into practice; even, that between 1950 and 1960 the diet of substantial sectors of the population deteriorated to well below medically recommended levels.[3]

The question they ask has even more force for the 1970s, where the research, despite the efforts of the professional pressure groups for the old and sick, has been equally complacent: 'How was it that politicians of all parties, commentators of all persuasions, "experts" in social enquiry, and professionals engaged in social work, should all have accepted so quickly and prematurely that poverty had become a memory of the past?'

Left behind in the boom

Because of what was assumed to be universal affluence, those who failed to 'achieve' became objects of pity, or derision. The chastening discovery of misery by the well-off during the wartime lowering of social barriers, the post-war anger, passion and commitment to change, evaporated into the sweet, comfortable haze of a complacent and affluent society. Instead of indignation there was now blame (and shame). A certain smugness replaced the need to do something. 'Something' was already being done by something called the Welfare State, whose real provisions were a great deal more modest than supposed by a public regaled with tales of housewives calling ambulances to do their shopping and being showered with wigs and glasses galore. At the underside of the aggressive, ambitious and successful society were the casualties of the Welfare State who were at fault for not being part of the general success.

According to the philosophers of the 'Never had it so good' society, it was the homeless' own fault when they were fleeced by a slum landlord, the sacked worker clearly did not deserve his employment in the first place, the deserted wife had failed as a mother and probably was not sufficiently attractive. The unmarried woman who nursed her demanding and ill mother, the family which made ends meet on low wages, the old couple valiantly starving because welfare 'is for people who are really poor', the disabled, the mentally subnormal, the war widows, the old who never left their darkened homes, were excluded from the main source of improved living standards because they were unable to take part in the productive life of the economy. The Welfare State abutted with the Nuclear Family: anyone outside its comfortable prison was, by definition, a problem.

The allowances they received were smaller in real value than supposed, probably a smaller percentage of average wages than in 1938, or even 1912. And their universality was, from the outset, undercut by tests and charges which further lowered their real value. Not only did the poor lack all sorts of private insurance and taxation benefits that the better off could use to buttress themselves in times of need but their entitlements were so complicated, hard to track down and surrounded with the aura of charity that many eligible people never claimed them. Baffled by forms or barred by pride, many of the most deserving soldiered on. It was, curiously, in the interests of both main political parties to exaggerate the extent of welfare and the equalisation of living standards brought about by progressive taxation: Labour to bolster its claims to social justice; the Tories to substantiate their dislike of any form of universal welfare. In 1958 the Director of the Conservative Political Centre, writing on the future of the Welfare State, described an imaginary system 'squandering public money on providing indiscriminate benefits for citizens, many of whom do not need them and some of whom do not want them'. No one liked admitting that social and medical services were as essential to modern society as public sewerage had been to the Victorian cities and for the same reason: the homeless, the disabled, the elderly and the unemployed were all inevitable results of the very social system that so cherised competition, thrust and aggression.

Instead Labour relinquished power with the sheer volume of its legislation concealing heavy political compromises. The 1945 drive to renew, to recreate and to plan was exhausted and outwitted. The Tories, rejoicing in the triumph of commercial ethics, while maintaining the main institutional changes, allowed the social equalisation of the immediate post-war years to openly polarise again into two, affluent nations, for rather than growth of the share of housing, education and health care going to manual workers and their families, what happened was that things improved for all, but much faster for those already better off. As Professor Titmuss has concluded:

> We know from fifteen years experience of the Health Service that the higher income groups know how to make better use of the service; they tend to receive more specialist attention; occupy more of the beds in better equipped and staffed hospitals; receive more selective surgery; have better maternity care, and are more likely to get psychiatric help and psychotherapy than the lower income groups – particularly the unskilled.[4]

Those whose medical and social needs were the greatest, living in declining housing with dwindling employment and overcrowded streets got the worst services rather than those their situation merited.

As so often with the Labour Party's ingenious schemes of social levelling which aim to secure social equality while leaving economic oligarchy intact, it was soon apparent that the upper classes managed to prosper, even in schemes designed to achieve the reverse.

Class and health: from birth to burial

It is often argued that to cavil about inequality according to class is to perpetuate a narrow-minded sectionalism. 'Why should the successful not enjoy reward,' we are told. But their success is contingent on someone else's failure. And while we might accept that a man with wealth is entitled to provide himself with a larger car, does the possession of cash alone make him deserve a longer life? Class inequality in health are matters of life and death in the final analysis and to justify its existence one must cold-heartedly believe that unskilled workers deserve to die younger, be shorter of breath or lose more of their children in child-birth. Just as the rich have become richer and the workers less poor, so the rich have become healthier and the poor less sick. But the less well off still suffer illness and make do with medical services which would be rejected bitterly by their betters. David Ennals summarised the evidence in a speech in March 1977:

To take the extreme example, in 1971 the death rate for adult men in Social Class V [unskilled workers] was nearly twice that of adult men in Social class I [professional workers] even when account had been taken of the different age structure of the two classes. When you look at death rates for specific diseases the gap is even wider. For example, for tuberculosis the death rate in Social Class V was ten times that for Social Class I; for bronchitis it was five times as high and for lung cancer and stomach cancer three times as high. Social class differences in mortality begin at birth. In 1971 neo-natal death rates – deaths within the first month of life – were twice as high for the children of fathers in Social Class V as they were in Social Class I. Death rates for the post neo-natal period – from one month up to one year – were nearly five times higher in Social Class V than in Social Class I.

Maternal mortality – down a long way from the figures of 40 years ago – shows the same pattern; the death rate was twice as high for wives of men in Social Class V as for those in Social Class I.

At age 5 Social Class I children are about an inch taller than

Social Class V children. About twice as many people reported long-standing illness which limited their activity in Social Class V as in Social Class I. The average number of days off work due to illness or injury was about six times greater in Social Class V than in Social Class I. Spells off work due to bronchitis were nearly four times greater for men in Social Class V than for Classes I and II; and for arthritis and rheumatism nearly six times greater. A survey showed in 1968 that 15 per cent of Social Class I adults had no teeth, while 47 per cent of Social Class V adults had no teeth. Finally, the male suicide rate in Social Class V men of working age was approximately twice that of men in Social Class I.[5]

The National Health Service . . . on the cheap

It is perhaps the existence of these two quite different levels of expectation and demand which helped to sustain another myth about the N. H. S.: that it was lavishly financed. It was quite possible for a metropolitan liberal to assume that the standard of care and the quality of equipment in the London teaching hospitals were general rather than exceptional. First, as regards financing, it is worth stating emphatically that the overwhelming proportion of N. H. S. funding in the post-war period came from direct taxation. A survey in 1972 suggested that 80 per cent of those interviewed still thought that the health service was financed from their stamp, which in fact now only produced 8 per cent of the sum. The N. H. S. is not free in any real sense, it is paid for by direct taxation of wages and salaries, and cuts or charges for it are equivalent to wage cuts. Although doctors sometimes contrive to give the impression that the health service is some magnificent act of personal generosity on their part, everthing they prescribe or advise, as well as their own wages, is financed by direct taxation.

The N. H. S. has also meant health on the cheap. The House of Commons Committee bent on uncovering abuse was forced to conclude: 'It is the opinion of our Committee that no Government has ever provided sufficient money to allow the Health Service to function and react to growing needs effectively.' And this echoes general, if inaudible, amazement at the relatively low spending on health by comparison with other countries. Until 1969, N. H. S. spending as a proportion of G. N. P. never exceeded 4.5 per cent, whereas in that year West Germany spent 5.7 per cent, the Netherlands 5.9 per cent, Sweden 6.7 per cent, the United States 6.8

per cent, and Canada 7.3 per cent.[6] Even allowing for the fact that some capital sums were 'shunted' into that total because of the sharp decline in spending required for tuberculosis control and some of the other communicable diseases, British spending was low and the annual estimates grew very slowly. In most Western countries health spending increased very briskly, at about 9 per cent per year, from the late 1960s, although the British proportion did move up (to about 5.2 per cent of G. N. P.) by the mid-1970s, total spending was still only one-third of American health-care expenditure.

Now some of this disparity can be explained by the sheer inefficiency of market-place health. The very high spending in North America reflects, not a concern for good health, but the power of a health empire, where doctors and hospitals see making money as a legitimate aspect of their profession and in the process are inevitably inclined to unnecessary referral, investigation and operation. Untrammelled clinical freedom does not need to more rational practice but the reverse, unnecessary investigations and operations which may lead to unnecessary deaths. Rates for the removal of the appendix are fairly equal as between Canada and England and Wales. But the removal of tonsils or the more serious procedure of cholecystectomy (removal of gall bladder), operations which depend a good deal on the initiative of the surgeon and are more controversial in worth, are three times more frequently performed in Canada where health insurance has been grafted on to a fee-for-service system: 20 per cent of Canadian doctors earned more than $50,000 in 1970. To quote a recent report:

> A US Senate Committee has said that between a quarter and a half of the £8,500 million spent on Medicaid is being wasted each year – a sum not far short of the total cost of the N. H. S. The man who directed the Senate investigation Senator Frank Moss of Utah, posed as a workman and visited a private health centre claiming he thought he might have a cold. He was given a complete medical examination, blood tests, X-rays, urine tests, a mis-diagnosis of a muscle spasm, treatment by a chiropractor and a number of prescriptions.[7]

One enterprising Chicago doctor became so proficient in dealing with his patients over the phone that he continued his practice while stationed in the army in the Deep South. Using long-distance calls and weekend passes, he treated 1190 patients in two months.[8]

In 1977 medicine in the United States is the single largest industry behind automobiles; by 1980 it will be out in front. With it will go private fortunes (Ross Perot's Electronic Data Systems of Dallas, say, who stand to supply the computer technology for the Medicaid and Medicare programme and will end up with the same stranglehold as the American Telephone and Telegraph Company enjoys in the field of communications) and unfettered advertising ('Within five years,' said Shirley Bonnem, marketing director of the Children's Hospital in Philadelphia, 'hospitals and doctors will be advertising freely. In ten years, maybe, they will do TV commercials'). In many public-health standards, the United States still remains below the British standards achieved with so much more modest but more democratically and efficiently planned resources.

In Britain's N. H. S. more confinements took place in hospital, more road accidents were treated successfully, more provision was made for industrial accidents, a great increase in the number of specialised diagnostic services was made available to G. P.s, whose list size shrank a little. But the main cause here has been the decade's long exploitation of the willingness of hospital workers, especially nurses, to put up with very low wages because of their vocational commitment to the service. The full extent of low pay, especially among junior doctors, was further concealed by the extensive use of migrant doctors, mainly from India and Pakistan, who by 1974 had come to make up 60 per cent of all senior house officers and 56 per cent of all registrars, more markedly in the unpopular regions and specialities. Sucked here in search of English higher degress and the blindness of the medical market, they staffed residential positions for which they are relatively less qualified. Their welcome presence has nevertheless disguised the real extent of under-financing. Without them the service would have openly collapsed. Yet the migrant doctors themselves were seldom given the promised education facilities to improve their linguistic and medical standards. Once again, 'training grades' were used to provide cheap and uncomplaining labour and received in return a rather perfunctory education.

And this uncomplaining devotion, which was in many ways its own worst enemy, also allowed an institutional meanness about buildings and resources to go unchallenged. The foundation of the National Health Service ushered in the slowest rate of hospital-building for two centuries. It is perhaps easier to appreciate quite how low average spending has been on the N. H. S. by direct comparison with the other social services: roughly half the schools and nearly half the houses have been built since 1948, only just a quarter of the hospitals. The majority of hospitals are pre-1914 whereas only one in six schools dates back that far.

Supply and demand

If the staff and patients became acclimatised to penny-pinching, on the other hand the suppliers of the service had access to a gigantic market. And where commercial principles came into conflict with the N. H. S., it was the former that appeared to triumph. Here, we are not simply referring to the well-known cases of pharmaceuticals' suppliers who were able to milk the N. H. S. by enormous excess charges from drugs sold at prices grotesquely at variance to their real cost, but to a whole range of suppliers from bed-pans to tea bags for which the N. H. S. was a gigantic and none too inquiring corporate purchaser.

Again the striking factor is the lack of national policy and clarity in the N. H. S.'s dealings with commercial supplying bodies and this is a function of the general growth of the service as a bureaucratic machine which, while under the nominal control of Parliament, is largely directed by an effectively self-appointed middle-class gerontocracy. The elements of popular control which had been so strong in the mining clubs have been largely extinguished. Now a member of the public hardly has an adequate complaints mechanism, let alone a say in the direction of the health service they pay for and upon which they have to depend in case of sickness. This has served to shield the service from any astringent criticism or assessment of its direction. The authorities often claim that the absence of complaints signifies general satisfaction with the system but it is more likely to evidence a numbed disinterest and passivity about even starting to ask for more or different health services.

Hierarchies rule

Hospitals, despite the N. H. S., remain spheres governed by people whose attitudes deprive patients of rights or opinions and whose power seems to get greater at each phase of the development of the health service. Ironically it is the doctors, and the more senior ones at that, bitter enemies of nationalisation, who have done best out of it, and the patients who have still further forfeited any say in what is perhaps the most fundamental of the social services their taxes buy. The co-operation, potential good will and devotion which the service attracts from the public is unique. What could have been achieved if its potential had ever been expressed is unknown, for it became swiftly bogged down in the swarm of professional self-aggrandisement and administrative inertia, more sensitive to the constant beckoning of the established powers and unworried by the inroads of commercial forces. And yet, ironically again, it has been the lowliest of the hospital hierarchy who have restarted, by their direct action about pay-beds and spending cuts, fundamental questioning about the direction and priorities of their service.

By default, money has tended to follow the lines of the old medical hierarchies, towards the centres of teaching medicine, and to reflect their concerns. Heart surgery is more exciting medically than an occupational health service, although the latter would do infinitely more for over-all health standards. Yet there is relatively little point in having specialised points of great expertise if the means of delivering it is neglected. Sudden advances in treatment methods are deprived of their potential value if the means to make early diagnoses of the condition do not exist. This intensely hierarchical set-up is constantly refuelled by the male offspring of doctors who bring with them an unchanging set of assumptions about rugby, medicine and the doctor's role they started imbibing in nappies (which is why they are so popular with the Medical School Dean's sense of eternal verity).

They are also, and perhaps this is the most stark example of the inequality of distribution which has arisen inside the N. H. S., failing to touch some of the most important causes of ill-health. Concern for healthy conditions at work, the site of 90 per cent of serious accidents, is so absent from the N. H. S. that its own hospitals are notoriously dangerous places to work and have been excluded from the safety regulations which cover the rest of industry. Apart from the special hazards which arise from radioactivity in X-ray departments, infection in pathology laboratories and chemical hazards in pharmacies, hospitals, because they are such outdated structures, are riddled with rudimentary health risks like asbestos and poor fire-guarding. How can such a service even begin to attempt to erase the causes of ill-health in private industry?

Women

Only five years ago a section with this title in a medical study would have been odd but the rise of the women's liberation movement makes it essential, if rather hard for a male doctor to write, for the women's movement has insisted on talking openly about the pressures on women which lie behind the stress, depression, 'minor ailments' and gynaecological problems which make women the most frequent users of doctors, hospitals and medicines. The struggle to bring up children as well as working, the pressure of the two jobs women are expected to cope with when husbands refuse to do housework or look after children when *they* come home from work, the loneliness of living in isolated homes in destroyed ugly developments, the ignorance of sexual anatomy which is considered proper to 'decent' women, the sense of disappointment and hollowness locked away in so many women's private psyches, all were invisible – considered normal – until large numbers of women began to protest and organise against them. This alone has altered the way doctors ought to think and alerted them to the masculine bias and deep-rooted assumptions which are so powerful in clinical medicine. The women's health movement challenges doctors to ask fundamental questions about the kind of medicine we have hitherto taken for granted. All those casual hysterectomies, quick diagnoses of depression, induced and interfering deliveries and buck-shot prescribing of tranquillisers, justified with some unspoken assumption about the inherent instability of the female intelligence, stand in need of review.

The renewed controversy over abortion law reform has proved the most emotive battlefield. The 1967 Act, generally supported by the exhaustive inquiry made in the Lane Report, has been subjected to considerable criticism and two major attempts, by the M. P.s James White and William Benyon, at restrictive amendment. The crux of their case, supported militantly by the powerful anti-abortion lobby, is that the provision for legal abortion on social grounds has been abused by permissive or even immoral doctors and commercial nursing homes, resulting in excessive terminations and the lowering of sexual standards. Their opponents, led by the Abortion Law Reform Association and the more radical National Abortion Campaign, argue that the rise in legal terminations represent the decline of the hazardous back-street abortion and the legitimate desire of women to exercise control over their own fertility. For them, and for me, abortion is an inevitable element in the medical spectrum of contraception and should be freely available, and early, at the request of the women rather than the behest of doctors, who are often rather poorly equipped to make this all-important decision on their own.

The campaign has been acrimonious and is far from over. This is not a suitable place to review the complex debate or detail the political campaign. But two challenges made by the campaign for the women's right to choose do throw light on the general state of the N. H. S. The first is their success in demonstrating the very wide regional variation in the availability of N. H. S. terminations, for the difficulties facing an unwillingly pregnant woman in Birmingham or Liverpool point yet again to the enormous individual powers vested in the individual consultant who is clearly able to block hospital terminations according to personal belief in the face of the wishes of women patients, general practioners or even their junior clinical staff.

The second, more optimistic, point is the evidence that many doctors, young and old, from consultant to trainee, do not wish to exercise this sort of ultimate judgement over what is essentially a personal rather than a clinical decision. The 500-strong Doctors for a Women's Choice on Abortion (D. W. C. A.), formed on the initiative of two women doctors in Edinburgh, have chosen to campaign not simply against the restrictive legislation (which has been consistently opposed by the main medical organisations, including the B. M. A. and the Royal College of Obstetrics and Gynaecology) but to divest doctors of their right to determine these matters and to place it emphatically in the hands of the woman who is contemplating termination. This resolution to confine medical authority to the strictly clinical sphere is a welcome sign of doctors' confidence that in voluntarily laying aside the social power attained by the profession they will be furthering the true interest of the patient and thus the best aims of medicine.

Radical women have pursued this stress on medical self-determination with groups and conferences aimed at dispelling the mystery with which many other areas of women's medicine are still surrounded, for the patient at least. Contraceptive methods, childbirth, vaginal infections, health education and diet have all been scrutinised and criticised. The fresh light cast by this searching inquiry ought to be taken seriously by all health workers who see their skills as a common property which ought to be as generally available as is possible rather than the private preserve of aloof professionals.

The missing dimension

However, to view the problems of the service simply in terms of unchallenged poverty, unequal access, skimped spending, undemocratic operation, masculine bias or out-of-date buildings, although each one of those factors has powerful effects, is to underestimate the problem. They add up to something more fundamental: a cheap but inefficient system exists which answers the needs of the individuals who stay in power and fails to tackle the major causes of ill-health. So although there has been a marked improvement in health care since the National Health Service, this has been a piecemeal rather than a planned process, where those areas which have the most disease still have the fewest doctors and facilities, and better-off patients manage mysteriously to cream off the best standards of treatment. Far from evaporating, poverty and ill-health have persisted, and even at the height of affluence an estimated six million people live on or below subsistence level; the old, the chronically ill, the handicapped, the widowed or orphaned, still tend to become locked into a vicious circle where shortage of money, poor diet and housing prevent recovery and illness cuts away at income. The scientific advances are still isolated in the centres of excellence and the medical concerns of the health service tend to follow doctors' interests rather than patients' needs. Prolonged under-financing was disguised by the willingness of N. H. S. workers to go on, out of a genuine sense of devotion as well as through their lack of trade-union experience, accepting very low wages for long and inconvenient hours. Many of the medical opportunities opened up by a national service, especially in the fields of preventative medicine and health education, were not explored. Many of the unattractive aspects of pre-N. H. S. medicine – private practice with N. H. S. facilities, the absolute power of consultants which many do not themselves relish, the dominance of the teaching hospitals, the underdevelopment of general practice – actually worsened.

None of this amounts to an argument against a national health service. The virtual collapse of market-place medicine in Italy or the persistently low standards of public health in North America should be a warning against any hoped-for return to the old system. But it was the wrong sort of nationalisation, its principles were not pursued consistently and it was leaking with the compromises built into its original structure. Although its radicalism was flawed from the start, radicals have often approached it with a protective sentimentality. They have hoped for more financial justice from national governments who out of office promise generosity but in power rely on a series of panaceas and commissions, most recently one on the reorganisation of the N. H. S., to solve what are much more fundamental problems.

The hospitals

'The N. H. S.,' said Dr David Owen when Minister of Health, 'still has an appalling legacy of old buildings.' I can still remember the sense of shock when, after six years as a medical student, I arrived at a hospital which had *not* been built in the nineteenth century. It was quite unnerving to work without the familiar gaunt Victorian arches and corridors, blackened iron fire-escapes, tea-coloured walls and cramped viewless offices. As a patient and a doctor my idea of hospitals was automatically that they were outdated, unsuitable and depressing and that a good deal of emotional effort needed to be spent on overcoming their physical discomfort. Nearly a quarter of British hospitals are over one hundred years old; they were very often built as workhouses and contain in their stark architecture a deliberate gloominess. Within these shells hospital architects have exercised a great deal of ingenuity in adding on units, inserting facades and attempting to redesign ward spaces. But anyone who works in British hospitals will be familiar with pioneering research projects that take place in Nissen huts, venereal units stuck away in out-houses rather less comfortable than public lavatories, and maternity clinics in clanking halls that echo every syllable passing between doctor and patient to the entire waiting queue, staring, tea-less and toy-less, into space.

The sprawling maze-like structure accumulated from the different phases of improvements and amalgamated uneasily by the old corridor structure of the original hospital would fox the most learned laboratory rat. It is a major task simply to prevent patients, visitors and new staff losing themselves. The point is not just that the hospitals are old and designed for a type of medicine no longer practised, but that their rambling, inefficient and gloomy structure creates a similar mentality in those who try and work in them. One becomes accustomed to cramped and dingy wards and accepts hospital medicine to be practised despite the buildings rather than with their aid. It is second nature to see patients taken to and from operating theatres across open yards, food travelling large distances from where it is cooked to the ward where it is served, inevitably cold and drab, and out-patients' waiting areas cramped and uncomfortable. One forgets how to protest and becomes quite hurt if others do.

Post-war hospitals

Not a single new hospital was built between 1948 and 1955 and only six were finished in the next ten years. One solitary general hospital was constructed in the first seventeen years of the N.H.S. and this has conditioned the outlook of a generation. It does much to explain quite how muted many who work in the health service are about conditions which other doctors or the lay public would consider outrageous. We have grown accustomed to soldiering on, usually fortified by a long-promised, oft-postponed and interminably discussed new district hospital. Instead consultants settle for an upgrading here, a facelift there and a new piece of technology which has to be wedged away in some corridor or cupboard; and this in turn aggravates the problem. Regular basic maintenance is inevitably neglected until it is a major undertaking in itself, and panic-stricken administrators, suddenly worried about the undoubted fire and safety risks of such unhealthily maintained hospitals, decide to close down the whole hospital, thus squandering what might be solid in the original structure and the money spent on the various piecemeal repairs and improvements over the years. Worst of all, it tends towards a medicine as ramshackle and second-rate as the buildings it is carried out in.

In the teaching hospitals themselves there is sufficient concentration of staff, enthusiasm and modern equipment to rise above the unsuitable buildings. In the hospital where I did my training it used to be the subject of a certain amount of wry pride that clinical research of world eminence was being carried out in crowded huts which would have been unacceptable as a carpenters' rest-room on a well-organised building site. And it is undoubtedly true that splendid mansions of North American medicine often house rather less eminent intellectual achievements. But in those hospitals on the borders of the empires, unvisited by senior staff except in office hours, permanently under-staffed and under high pressure with low prestige, morale and medical standards soon sag. And in the large hospitals for the mentally ill and handicapped, conveniently isolated in luxurious looking rural follies, standards dropped to the level of a public scandal.

The asylums

The conditions in the asylums of Britain was only exposed publicly in the mid-1960s when the public was first forced to face up to the long gaunt wards where elderly patients shuffled in faded, shabby, ill-fitting clothes without their own toothbrush or teeth, let alone personal possessions, and eked out a miserable life with a handful of staff who could do little more than escort them to the lavatories and stun them with the chemical equivalent of the old straitjacket.

Even then, although some doctors had been arguing for years that the conditions of treatment in mental hospitals were causing more mental illness than they were curing, it took the proven cases of brutality by mental nurses at Ely new Cardiff to begin serious public investigations into standards in the long-stay hospitals. The studies showed that the extent of reform was still slight, mainly through problems of staffing and lack of finance. According to the memoirs of Richard Crossman, the Department of Health were well aware of the problem but quite prepared to hush it up.[9] Crossman's Hospital Advisory Service, whose inspection visits were forewarned and far from penetrating, still found a dismaying picture. The 1969–70 report, which concentrated on the long-stay hospitals found:

> in far too many, nursing resources are so slight compared with the number of patients to be cared for that little more than basic care can be provided, [that the older hospitals for mentally handicapped] are grossly overcrowded; 50 or more patients on wards intended for 40 is a common finding. There is often no room for lockers, or personal possessions, too few toilets and too few staff even to give elementary training. It is not surprising that under these conditions the hospitals were afflicted with outbreaks of dysentry, infective hepatitis and other infections.[10]

Even those hospitals which had tried to modify the barn-like structures of the old asylums had often been unsuccessful; 'some modern wards strike a singularly harsh, forbidding and clinical note, with relatively large bare areas and large dormitory spaces, now generally unacceptable if the formation of small groups and homely atmosphere is needed'.

As well as being common sense, it is now proven by the research of child psychiatrists like Kushlick that the attainments of mentally backward children improve in proportion to the amount of in-dividual attention they get. Small groups with continuous nursing contact encourage an inquiring response to the outside world. Uniformity and rote performance of daily duties at the lavatory, table and sink, in squads marshalled by a nurse who has literally no time for individuals, drives the child back to hide in the protection of his silent, inner self. And yet out of national meanness we tolerate institutions and force conditions on the staff who try to work in them which we would never tolerate for our own children if they were, by ill luck, to suffer from Down's syndrome or cerebral palsy.

It is, above all, in the old asylum buildings that house the elderly mentally ill that capital needs to be spent to undo decades of neglect, let alone to create hospitals for the future which will be capable of serving us in another thirty years' time. A coat of paint is an insult rather than an upgrading when what is wanted immediately are new toilets plumbed in or the replacement of a bed-pan washer that is always out of order, and what is really required is an entirely new, thoughtfully designed and custom-built unit. And yet, apart from a periodical *exposé* and pious editorials in a Sunday newspaper, people prefer to forget about these kind of problems unless they are directly concerned. We confine our indignation to buying charity Christmas cards. Yet how a society treats its members who are at the end of their lives, who have fought its wars and made its wealth is surely the measure of its degree of civilisation. In this respect we lag behind the naked tribesmen we choose to call 'primitive' but who would never countenance the way the infirm old in institutions can still die: 'Elderly patients suffer many inevitable indignities but should at least be able to wash in privacy, excrete in privacy and die in privacy. Too often these take place in view of others on the ward', reported the Hospital Advisory Service, without comment.

The modern hospitals

In the late 1960s and early 1970s capital spending devoted to hospital building increased to reach a peak in 1972 of £393 million and between 1966 and 1975, seventy-one new hospitals were either completed or started. But since 1973 a very sharp reduction in capital spending due to public expenditure cuts has reduced the new starts very dramatically and many of the hospitals constructed during the burst of building are unable to find the revenue to staff and run their newly constructed premises. Only fourteen major projects were started in 1975 and in the following year the Minister predicted that 'until at least 1980 the capital building programme will be at a level substantially lower than that obtaining over the past few years'. Almost the only schemes to survive are those linked directly to teaching hospitals. This means that many of the long-expected hospitals will simply not materialise, and people hanging on by the skin of their teeth in medically condemned buildings, whether they are teaching hospitals like St Mary's in Paddington or country district hospitals long overburdened by a rising population, as in Hemel Hempstead, will now have to abandon all hope and learn to live with what they have got.

In the process a considerable amount of money has been made and time wasted by private consultants who have done preliminary surveys and design work and in some cases knocked down existing facilities and purchased and cleared new sites only to have the project scuppered. The Department of Health and Social Security (D. H. S. S.) has appeared to favour at different times three completely different types of hospital: the large 1200-bed district hospital beloved of the 1969 Bonham Carter Committee; the 800-bed community hospital favoured by the Department in the early 1970s; and the 500-bed nucleus hospital currently in vogue. All sorts of arguments rattle backwards and forwards between the consultants and administrators who debate these matters but it takes no advanced statistical research to note that the hospitals become smaller and cheaper at each rethink. Here there is a real danger that, for the financial convenience of the D. H. S. S., once radical ideas, such as the small, G. P.-run community hospital, might be adopted as a modern-sounding euphemism for what should be seen as cuts in promised and needed public hospitals. It is also worth noting that many of the most prestigious hospitals that have been finished are beset with basic design deficiencies which arise from the very long gestation period and the remoteness, as always, of the planners from those who will use the service.

Design magazine noted:

> There was once an intelligent theoretical reason for the structural form of Hampstead's Royal Free Teaching District General Hospital. Eighteen years and £20.5m later, it is apparent that its ingenious but rigid circulation and service plan was the starting point for a design disaster which has infected many aspects of the finished job. The Royal Free is the newest hospital in Britain, but it was years out of date before it admitted its first patient.[11]

More important, the size and location of the finished new hospitals often worsens rather than improves the national distribution of medical resources. The Royal Free in Hampstead is situated in the most affluent and healthy part of North London, while hospital facilities in the North-west London industrial belt and in East London are being closed. In the acute hospitals themselves the pattern of care has altered. Since the foundation of the N. H. S. the length of stay in hospital has fallen steadily from the 1949 average stay of forty-nine days until it is more like eight days in the acute hospitals today. This statistic is often cited as proof of the hospital service's efficiency, by industrialists unhappy at the lack of ready medical equivalents to share and dividend prices with which to measure the N. H. S.'s 'output'. And it is probably true that this statistic depends a little on better-organised laboratory investigation and co-ordination and some decentralisation of authority. The service can no longer afford to keep a patient in bed for another week to await the consultant's round and the ordering of a few more extra tests to keep up the appearance of a full ward.

Hospital morale

However, the implications of this more rapid turnover are distressing. It has increased substantially the work-load required of hospital ward and laboratory staff, and decreased the chances to build up friendly and human relationships with patients. Impersonality is inevitable when the object of the exercise becomes the speed with which a patient can be safely sent home. This is especially frustrating because of the way that hospital work is always advertised as worth while and rewarding even though it permits less and less involvement and reward. Nurses in the 1973 strike often complained of this and the associated problem of under-staffing, worse at night, and skimped training, rather than the strictly cash issue. A Hackney doctor said:

I wanted to become a doctor for all the usual sorts of reasons. Feeling that it was a worthwhile job, wanting to help people, professional status. . . . What I found out when I started practising medicine was that the problems I was presented with as a doctor just couldn't be solved by me, however good I was. Say the people who get depressed because they live in really bad conditions, people who take overdoses. All I could do was pump their stomach, keep them in hospital for 24 hours, discharge them again as 'non-suicidal' and then wonder why they did it all over again in a week's time.

A radiographer who left the profession complains:

> after an extensive technical training, many radiographers find
> themselves pushing buttons and adjusting dials according to a
> duplicated sheet of exposure levels while patients are shuffled in
> and out as if on a production line. The amount of patient contact
> varies, but in a routine X-ray department it is minimal: 'Breathe in.
> Hold your breath.' Click. 'Breathe out. Good. Next please.'

For the consultant who usually only sees the in-patient on two or
three occasions, when all the preliminary ground work has been laid
by the house staff, an increased turnover of patients probably
increases job satisfaction. But to achieve it, the houseman has the
unpleasant task of 'booting out' the least ill surgical patients while the
arrivals for the next list wait their turn with a cup of tea in the sister's
office. At the general practitioner's end there is an increase of
problems with wound infections, post-operative pain and poor
healing. Very often pressure on the wards delays even the notification
of discharge dates and current drugs available, and a full summary of
what has happened in hospital can often take several weeks to
materialise. More patients, especially with abdominal pain, are
discharged without a diagnosis and many patients whose home
circumstances are not suitable for convalescence are deprived of a
more gentle hospital recovery. Such is the tempo of investigation that
many patients return home utterly exhausted. If the discharge is
rushed, and this is more and more often the case, there is no time to
warn relatives adequately, let alone the relevant social and nursing
services.

Turnover mania is accompanied by a marked tendency among
hospital doctors to use the term 'social admission' in a purely
pejorative sense to describe a case where poor housing or lack of
relatives is a factor in the need for a hospital bed. In practice the tag
often conceals an incomplete clinical examination, but the marked
dislike exhibited by some hospital doctors towards certain categories
of patient reflects an unfortunate narrowing of their conception of a
hospital. Too often it has become merely a production line of
interesting acute cases. Patients not falling into such a category
become instead an unfortunate 'disposal' problem to be dealt with by
lower orders. The structure and the professions again assert their
tendency to put their needs before those of the patient.

This leads to the larger question of the undue influence of the acute hospitals on the service as a whole. The hospitals take the lion's share of spending, although there is a sharp disparity between spending per patient in the acute hospitals and the long-stay units housing the old, mentally disturbed and sub-normal. Indeed, given the present budget, the advances in transplant surgery and nuclear medicine have been made at the expense of generally lower standards in maternity and emergency medicine. And the acute hospital represents and owes its prestige to the merging of clinical medicine at its zenith with modern medical technology and pharmacology and the university system through which undergraduate medicine is financed. However sympathetic its practitioners have, diplomatically, become towards their colleagues in general practice, the very nature of the medicine and research they practise resists taking primary care very seriously. The G. P. is glimpsed at the drug company dinners, perfunctory letters are exchanged, a junior might have to deal with a late-night pre-admission call, but often that is as far as it goes.

The pyramid of hospital power

Inside the hospital, behind its neoclassical facade, lies an even more marked pyramid of power with the wealthy, white, male consultant at its pinnacle and Asian and Caribbean women cleaners, cooks and ward nurses toiling away, underpaid and under-appreciated at the base. This highly developed hierarchy, with its intricate snobberies and subtle racial and sexual wars, corrodes the possibility of genuine co-operation upon which any effective healing depends and over-plays the importance of medical actions made by doctors at the expense of nursing, diet and hygiene in a way the classical physicians would have found bewildering. The hierarchical system is not simply a comic anachronism, suitable for *Doctor in the House* films and requiring six separate grades of canteen and cutlery, but it creates its own problems which distort the patient care which everyone professes is the ultimate aim of the operation. In this respect, at least, teaching hospitals are the worse offenders.

The ultimate power is still possessed by the consultant as the head of the clinical team. The specialities themselves still tend to rank in prestige according to potential earnings in private practice rather than its over-all social utility or medical challenge. The teaching hospitals produce a medical profession modelled on a template which no longer fits the jig of reality. Medical schools have resisted educational democracy most staunchly; a recent Parliamentary

Question elicited a figure of 33 per cent of medical students from public schools, which are attended by only 3 per cent of the population, and a further 13 per cent from grant-aided schools, and a more recent survey of Birmingham University Medical School confirms the over-representation of the offspring of doctors and the disturbing fact that applicants connected by birth to the hospital appeared to require lower examination results.[12]

Within nursing there is a similar caste system with well-off girls with petal-pink complexions still training at the London teaching hospitals but otherwise few working-class English girls attracted to a job which demands terrible hours for very poor money under antiquated discipline. Instead in the non-prestige big hospitals nursing staff have traditionally been women from Ireland and the West Indies, with Malaysian, Asian and African migrants making up more and more of the woman power in the 1960s. All training nurses have their labour exploited. They have to work harder than the full-time qualified staff, right up to their examinations and are often too tired to study or attend to the lectures properly.

The most elementary rights to privacy, telephones and an adult social life are forfeited; nurses can request evenings they want off but have to fall in with the ward sister's time-table. Unqualified staff are consistently landed with responsibility beyond their real experience, particularly at night; this is by no means exceptional. The qualified night staff are forced to rotate through the wards hoping to be in the right place at the right time, and administrators play a nightly chess game to try and divide their sparse forces according to the current nursing needs of the patients. Sickness absence, which is higher than average among hospital staff because of the sheer pressure of the work, can punch a hole through the best-planned night provision. For every hospital that admits frankly that it has to close wards because of staff shortage, there must be several who are getting away with a calculated risk which would probably horrify the senior staff who unfortunately do not see the hospital at night. A teaching hospital which has a clamour of staff falling over each other in the week can be a medical shell at weekends with registrars living out, leaving junior doctors, agency casualty nurses and locum housemen holding the fort.

State-enrolled nurses are particularly exploited. They get a second-rate education for a qualification which is only valid in England. Yet as students they do the bulk of manual work on the wards with very little recognition, job security or prospects. And that work is demanding, both physically and emotionally, requiring concentration and precision as well as sheer brute strength and stamina. Dire punishment awaits the ward nurse if her tally of pain-killers is inaccurate or observations are running behind, even though the drugs are harmless and non-addictive and the doctors do not always bother to read the charts. In medicine as in life it is the male sex that makes the decisions and the female that carries them out. The hospital hierarchy is one of sex as well as income and class. On ward rounds it is still only the sister or staff nurse who speaks, and then only when spoken to. The cynicism with which the labour of women migrants has been used in British hospitals is signified by the government's withdrawal of work permits to migrant nurses once they qualify, thus refusing them the only work to which their newly qualified but now useless status equips them. The contrast between the illusory glamour of Nightingale and Kildare and the reality of a ward of ill patients to nurse single-handed on Saturday night is measured by the number of nurses who leave the profession, now a staggering 30 per cent a year.

Still further down the scale are those ancillary workers whose essential contribution to the well-being of the patient has only recently been acknowledged, let alone rewarded adequately. Hospital porters, cleaners and cooks are the lowest paid of the low paid, and only make ends meet by working levels of overtime which is unhealthy for them and their patients. Yet without their toil, the most sophisticated surgery and high-powered clinician come to a stop. Here again, the tendency to overemphasise what can be achieved by doctors tends to undervalue the importance of good diet, hygienic surroundings, rest and friendly company. Instead nurses are rushed off their feet trying to carry out the doctors' instructions and sisters' requirements. Often the only person who has time to get to know the patient is a passing ward orderly or clerk.

Dazzled by the gleaming technology, we too seldom ask of hospitals more basic questions. Are they frightening, is it easy to find someone to talk to, is the food tempting and nutritious, is it easy to rest, to recover at your own pace, or to die with dignity? Instead we have 'the patient is always wrong' syndrome and the person most concerned with a decision is the last to be told about it. This attitude can extend from an unnoticed inhumanity to what amounts to deliberate cruelty.

The 'patient is always wrong'

My first experience of hospital was during long childhood stays as a sufferer from, first, tuberculosis and then polio. In the middle of my memories of the kindness of the nurses and the other patients, the presence of doctors seemed occasional and special, arriving in troupes after a morning of feverish but usually unnoticed scrubbing and polishing of the ward, to discuss the progress of one part of your body while you, rather embarrassed, stared at the ceiling, tried not to cry and pretended not to be getting in the way. After they had safely left the ward (doctors are always 'busy' and flap their coats as if a life-saving event requiring their presence lies around every corridor corner), patients would confer about what was decided, most importantly whether there was any chance of discharge. The junior nurses would join in the guess-work. I grew to understand that the patient was usually wrong about everything, that once you got your bed-pan you would probably be stranded, perched on it for an hour, that the patients had only the amount of dignity, status and rights they could squeeze from the system, and we all stayed in such ignorance, not from malice but because it was nobody's job to explain, except the houseman, who was half asleep anyway. We were not people, we were a 'tib and fib', a 'Charnley', and 'two fractured necks or femurs'.

This kind of atmosphere was investigated painstakingly and reported on by a bevy of campaigners and committees in the 1960s. It results, not from personal malice or organisational incompetence, but from the whole system of acute hospital medicine as it has grown up. Even the measured official language of the time reveals quite how rigid and unsuitable the ward regimes had often become. In 1961 the Powell Report noted that 'Rest is an essential part of a patient's treatment, yet it is becoming progressively more difficult to rest in hospital . . . the patient is called upon to endure a marathon beginning far too early in the morning and ending late at night'. A parent and some enlightened pediatricians forced action on the unnecessary suffering of young children in hospital, crying, as I so clearly remember, ourselves to sleep at night with our nurses in tears at their inability to comfort us. Yet it took the campaigning work of James Robertson and the example of doctors like Dermot MacCarthy even to establish the desirability of parents staying with young children for more than the regulation visiting hour.

Child-birth as illness

The maternity service, which at the doctors' insistence, was increasingly hospitalised, was and is still justly criticised for splintering and spoiling the most joyous moments of birth with bossiness and production-line insensitivity. In 1973, 95 per cent of births took place in hospital compared with 60 per cent a generation ago. Between 1965 and 1975 the induction rate has risen from 15 per cent to 33 per cent and the forceps rate from 8 per cent to 11 per cent. The Caesarean section rate has remained at 5 per cent. These figures mean only half of all women are allowed to have their babies born naturally. Duly blasted with an enema, pubic hair razored, stunned with Pethidine and surrounded by nurses bellowing 'Just relax', a new baby's entry into this world takes place in pandemonium. For the mother, too often birth is a numb and scared agony that afterwards she does her best to drive out of her mind. The distraction, companionship and simple familiarities so normal at home suddenly become foreign. Child-birth becomes instead some kind of dread condition from which fathers, Englishmen anyway, have the decency to keep well away. Reporting in 1961 on the problems created by poor maternity facilities, the government publication *Human Relations in Obstetrics* warned:

> Sanitary and bathing facilities have become inadequate therefore, but the most important is the deficiency in first stage and labour wards. In some hospitals patients have to be left in open wards until the very last moment before being transferred into the labour ward. Midwives working under such conditions may become harassed and have less time for common courtesies.

Some hospital authorities, obviously believing a pregnant woman is inevitably unbalanced, refused to distribute the report, thereby proving the point made by the Cranbrook Report that 'We received the general complaint that there was too little regard in many hospitals for the personal dignity and emotional condition of the woman during pregnancy and childbirth. It was in this respect that the hospital as a place of confinement was compared most unfavourably with the home.'

Florence Nightingale, who spent most of her life handling facts, figures and plans, still understood that their object was the comfort of the sick and suffering. In 1859 she wrote: 'Apprehension, uncertainty, waiting, expectation, fear of surprise, do a patient more harm than any exertion. Remember he is face to face with his enemy all the time, having long imaginary conversations with him.' Yet nowadays when morale is mentioned, it is always the morale of the doctors, and it usually means they want more money. Staff have become more rather than less remote with the growing bureaucratisation of nursing. The increased division of medical labour means more and more medical experts extract blood, take pictures, inject dyes, measure, galvanise, manipulate. They all glance at the growing wad of notes to ascertain the cases's name, smile fixedly and say, 'Now, just relax, Mrs So and So', before beginning their work. Questions get only the most vague answers, yet the patient who presses his enquiry further is regarded as something of a menace. Patients go from beginning to end of a prolonged investigation, told little more than 'a bit too much acid on the tummy', or 'Stones'. They would probably require more precision from the mechanic who overhauls their car: 'Departmentalism . . . is more given to silence than communication. Silence from those in authority, from doctor, sister, nurse, administrator, clerk, technician and so on often means a want of imagination; silence consents to fear among those who have great need for explanation and reassurance', writes Richard Titmuss. [13]

This distance and mystery about procedures which have often been stripped of the really skilled elements by automation is a defence, but it further accentuates the patient's passivity and enlarges the gap between the high-technology medicine of the hospital and the social poverty of the home. In East London, one of the highest mortality rates in Britain is situated only half a mile from one of the most scientifically sophisticated units for the new-born in the country. Between them is a social chasm bridged by nothing more than a discharge note and an answering service. The problem of human relations in a hospital highlights the need to bring the hospital – as a social institution rather than a garage for bodies – back into society where it properly belongs. It has become too isolated and it needs to return to the community to take its lead and measure its success. As the Trades Council of Bethnal Green wrote:

> While it is reassuring to know that the very best in specialised treatment is available in the London Hospital we are worried about the extent to which highly sophisticated techniques may be developing at the expense of a satisfactory level of primary care. In a Borough with an aging population, a high morbidity rate and

birth rate, the local demands on the Hospitals are particularly for adequate gynaecological care as against some of the specialised services available at the London.[14]

As in Latin America, where medical prestige mongering results in the import of a kind of 'advanced' medicine still more irrelevant, this gulf is even more horrific. In Buenos Aires doctors are playing about with cardiac surgical units costing tens of thousands of dollars while new-born babies die in the precincts of the hospital for lack of decent milk.

Till death do us part

'It may seem a strange principle to enunciate as the very first requirement in a hospital that it should do the sick no harm', wrote Florence Nightingale. But nowhere is the principle disregarded more callously than at the point of death itself, nowhere else are the interests of the patients so unregarded. Medicine exists to save life not to prolong death. It has, however, created hospitals which are the hardest places in society in which to die with dignity. For my first year as a doctor, I sprinted half-dressed, half-asleep twice a week down a 600-yard corridor to attend to cardiac arrests. Dream-like, in front or behind, other doctors panted and bounced, the trolleys of equipment clanged, the buzzers squawked. Charging into darkened wards, we woke the patients, pummelled the dying one, jerked them inches off the bed with electric shocks, wrestled with their mouths to find a way down with an air-tube, cracked ribs, tried to interpret E. C. G. squiggles and titrate the right amount of drugs to elicit a response. Sometimes it was more like the experiments we had done with acetyl choline and frogs' muscle or stained physiology benches than medicine. Yet it was only on the night when a fairly fit patient had a heart attack, just from watching what we were up to, that it occurred to me to question the wisdom of what we were doing; for, while every effort can and should be devoted to monitoring and reviving patients in units equipped for intensive care, the kind of indiscriminate, ineffective invasion we carried out, which we wholeheartedly conceived as solely for the patient's good, was in fact depriving the dying of the last shred of dignity in order to give us a little practice and a little false prestige. None of this is to argue that we should abandon or relent our development of medical science, but we need to sharpen its focus, take more seriously its implications and applications. We need to ask honestly, every time, whether its net result enhances the doctor's prestige or the patient's well-being, for these are by no means the same thing.

4
Primary care

The family doctor is most people's first experience of the N. H. S. Nine out of ten patients who contact the N. H. S. are seen by about 25,000 G. P.s, under half the total medically qualified personnel. The G. P.s are the most myth-encrusted creatures in the service. They are supposed to practise in custom-built local-authority health centres according to Section 21 of the National Health Service Act which states: 'It will be the duty of every local health authority to provide, equip and maintain and staff health centres.'

They are contracted to provide a twenty-four-hour service to their flock but 8000 use profit-making night answering services where, after a suitable delay for re-routing calls, a cruising night doctor attends to those who inconveniently fall sick out of office hours. They are responsible for providing care all year round; a G. P. on a breathing machine after a heart attack is still technically responsible for his 2500 patients. The G. P.s like to think that they provide continuous care but in fact mainly see patients at times of illness. G. P.s are attributed by many consultants with a mediocrity, which is unfair, and by the public with a specialised grasp of all aspects of medicine, which they could never obtain. Even the touch of personal intimacy with their patients can only be obtained by an advanced sneak at the envelope of notes the individual medical records kept for every person in Britain, a major achievement in itself.

Almost any survey of G. P.s contradicts the next survey, and most of the definitions of their role are hopeless. At best the G. P. is a general physician with special skill in preventative and chronic medicine and experience of domiciliary practice, at worst a snap diagnostician with a telephone.

Medicine's cottage industry

What is undisputed is that this crucial section of medicine, whose organisation shapes people's access to and expectations of more specialised medicine, has changed relatively little since 1949 and has benefited least from the technical advances of medical science. 'The industrial revolution has passed general practice by; it remains a cottage industry, under-organised, under-capitalised and over-worked', said Professor Brotherton in 1963, and some of those cottages are still pretty ill-equipped.

In 1949 the B. M. A.'s shortsighted concern was aimed at preserving private practice for those who could afford it, leaving the state to insure the doctor against many patients' inability to pay. Their insistence on the fictional independence conferred by the beloved capitation scheme allowed the specialists to steal the gravy and the hospitals, and left primary practice locked in its own, partly self-imposed backwardness. The main change was in the relative prosperity of different G. P.s. Doctors who dealt with long lists in working-class areas moved from quite a mean living to relative affluence, whereas those G. P.s mainly in private practice with perhaps a handful of servants taken on as insurance patients found their erstwhile private patients joining the N. H. S. in droves and themselves very much less well off.

Either way the compromise system of payment positively encouraged inefficiency and rewarded low standards. It was better to take on a big list and do the bare minimum from basic premises than to restrict the numbers, lengthen the time available for each patient, and improve the facilities. Doctors in general practice became more rather than less separated from hospitals and each other; subconsciously one's fellow G. P. still led to criticism, competition, or both. Practising alone, clinical standards almost inevitably sink and slumber, finding accommodation with the realities of time and possibility rather than the organised thoroughness drummed into us at teaching hospital but plainly impossible in the trench war of general practice.

When the premium is on quantity not quality why bother? Why examine a chest with all the intricate tapping and touching and listening you impressed the examiners with, when all the old boy is asking for is another bottle of 'the mixture'? 'A well-trained man will throw over the hardwon disciplines of clinical training and accept the stultifying limitations of general practice . . . such acceptance of bad conditions has a stultifying effect', wrote a New Zealand doctor who was violently upbraided for his forthright survey of general-practice standards in 1950.[1]

Dr Collings found a jungle of premises, supervised by practitioners he divided into mercenaries and missionaries. He found small, cold and inhospitable surgeries, examination couches littered with records, instrument cupboards like museums of past interests, speculum rich in dust, and the chemicals at the sink of purely ornamental value. Working single-handed was offered as the excuse but he considered it little more than a convenient rationalisation for low standards. Examinations were usually confined to the offending organ and even then were cursory. 'With conditions as they are,' Collings thought bluntly, refresher courses 'would do as much good as an injection of adrenaline does with a patient with terminal heart failure.'

Conditions of practice

Thirteen years later, primary care had not succumbed but was still operating from premises which dated from the days when G. P.s strode about waiting for the pneumonia crisis to be resolved. Cartwright and Marshall found that in working-class areas 80 per cent of doctors' surgeries were built before 1900 and only 5 per cent since 1945.[2] Most were still converted shops with a bare waiting-room, tattered copies of *Woman's Own*, hard chairs and a few mouldering anti-smoking posters. Another survey of industrial practices found one in three had no receptionist or lavatory. A majority of premises still lacked adequate changing-rooms, which not only inconveniences the patient but effectively debars methodical physical examination.

The amalgamation of individual principals into group practices proceeded slowly, and although it lifted the inhuman pressure of night visiting, often it was a merger of the bad elements as well as the good. The G. P., by hanging on so grimly to a fictional independence and the status of a small shopkeeper, was in no position to adapt to change. Although the G. P. tended to attribute the low level of equipment, skill and morale to the public's abuses or the state's encroachment, it really lay in the under-capitalisation of the primary sector, the limited access and liaison with paramedical and social-work staff, the lack of custom-built premises and the sheer absence of time for reflection and education. Nothing interferes wih clear thought quite like the three-minute cascade of patients whose demands are as various as their faces and which switch in moments from the terminal cancer to the fictitious sore throat.

Health centres

The health centres had been conceived to solve this problem, to sustain clinical standards by spreading the work-load, linking other staff, and encouraging a degree of self-specialisation. Ten were opened in 1948, but by 1969 there were only eighty-seven, painfully slow progress for a service which was supposed to be seen as a duty for local authorities. The number of group practices has increased quite markedly; but it is by no means clear whether the medicine in group practices has altered or simply merged. Their aim was not just administrative convenience but to alter the range of medicine and the roles of those who delivered it. The potential of a properly designed, modern and attractive centre which provides a working base for doctors, dentists, nurses, health visitors and social workers is that it could genuinely become a centre for health. There would be sufficient skills pooled to avoid unnecessary and long-delayed excursions to hospital consultants and a large-scale operation would allow the basic laboratory investigations to be carried out both quickly and to high standards. The centre could be staffed at night to offer emergency callers personal advice and, if necessary, immediate access to relevant personal medical records. It could become a community centre where local people felt they had a right to attend and where they were welcome when they were well for screening and advice that went wider than what is narrowly defined as 'medical'. It could be the basis for services which patients themselves could help arrange: play-schools, nurseries, physiotherapy, help during convalescence, and specialist lay groups of fellow sufferers, say people trying to lose weight or stop smoking, who could support each other. Naturally and almost imperceptibly attitudes to health could be altered, and health education and medical self-knowledge become a reality.

With these centres well established, hospitals could indeed insist on stricter referrals, better case summaries from G. P.s which transmitted their full social knowledge, and they could discharge earlier with safety. They could perhaps exchange personnel fruitfully instead of just as a stop-gap, with a hospital specialist taking an occasional health-centre clinic and the G. P.s working a session or two in their special interest at the hospital. Health centres could have unclogged

the hospitals of the cases which were otherwise drawn to them by
default, and could have really developed their unique expertise.
Patients could recover a voice and some measure of sovereignty over
their own health care.

Domestic midwifery could begin a genuine revival, not with G. P.s
whose knowledge of abnormal midwifery is so sketchy that their best
contribution to averting catastrophe was to arrive late, but with
obstetrically experienced G. P.s committed to decent ante-natal care,
home delivery, proper care of the new-born and democratic co-
operation with a midwife sharing the same premises. There would no
doubt have been new sorts of problems, but since it was never tried we
will not know what they are. The 'lynch-pin' of health centres was
missing from the start, so it is little wonder that hospital and G. P.
pulled so far apart from each other.

The collapse of the health-centre policy is conventionally attributed to a reluctance of existing general practitioners to relinquish
their individual premises. However, talking more carefully to doctors
who have been conveniently written off as unco-operative, often by
Labour Councils looking for an excuse for their own meanness, it is
more often the case that initial enthusiasm was destroyed by paucity
of finance, long and then still longer delays, and an evident lack of
commitment by local authorities to anything but the most rudimentary schemes. Very often the G. P.s simply settled for the devil they
knew.

The G. P.'s charter

Instead, by the mid-1960s, the G. P.s' volume of work and financial
reward, quite besides larger clinical problems, had reached a crisis.
This crisis was partly about pay but G. P.s should not be attributed *en
bloc* with the money-obsessed image of the B. M. A. The *General
Practitioner* rightly observed in 1965 that ' the sooner the Ministry of
Health and the BMA realise that what the vast majority of general
practitioners is interested in is service, and the means whereby they
can give this service to their patients, the sooner the citizens of this
country receive the medical care to which they are entitled'. And the
B. M. A. in one of its occasional moments of perception stated:

The public at large and the Minister of Health should realise that
this discontent lies deep. The medical profession too should realise,
in fact does realise, that this discontent is only in part due to the

mechanics of the health service. It is caused as much by the rapidly changing position that the general practitioner faces today with medical science far outstripping in its discoveries and application what he was taught at his medical school ten or even five years ago. . . . The GP has to get back into the mainstream of clinical life.

The crisis was really about the failure to devise the means to deliver medical care at the speed its potential was expanding. In the furnaces of the teaching hospitals great things were happening as the G. P.s attempted to stoke up their own medical boilers with back-issues of the *Lancet* and teach-yourself guides to electro-cardiography.

The Government produced the 'G. P.'s Charter', a collection of minor reforms. The curious arrangement by which G. P.s were, on their own insistence, still financed was improved. More capital funds were made available and practice improvement and surgery expenses were better compensated. Links with hospitals were formally established through a programme of postgraduate teaching centres. The rate of health-centre building was speeded up, that is until the country ploughed into the next trough of economic crisis. Training courses for general practice were established, the Royal College of General Practice, brain-child of a handful of pioneers, took on real authority.

These measures staved off the crisis, but it did not solve it. For some doctors it meant that for the first time in their professional life they were reasonably well off. For keener young doctors there was now a route to general practice that took training seriously, not just as the second-best option when you gave up hope on the hospital career ladder. In some centres and groups, a new spirit of co-operation between staff was established. But all too often the substance did not alter. Pioneer health centres merely confirmed the backwardness of the rest. Some of the trainee schemes were a way of ensuring that unpopular junior posts were filled rather than providing G. P.s with education. Some doctors in groups still did not even talk to each other, let alone to the social worker.

Casualty departments took up more and more of the burden of primary care. While one learns to be suspicious, I cannot disbelieve *all* the tales that I have been told in accident units, of non-examining G. P.s, unattended answering services, closed lists, and appointments' systems which seem designed to avoid seeing patients. The contact with the hospital has not been improved dramatically by the fact that some of the local G. P.s attend periodic drug company lunches in the hospitals while half-listening to one of the consultants on his favourite hobby-horse. Referral letters still rarely cover more than one side of note-paper, seem to pride themselves on illegibility and consider it a proper challenge to the admitting officer's skill to divulge as little information as possible. And the discharge notes have grown correspondingly distant and curt, designed more for hospital records than the practitioner's use except to fold into the typed bundle in the records' envelope.

If a hospital doctor does get past the answering service, or a G. P.'s enquiry penetrates the wiles of hospital switchboards, only the most basic information is exchanged. When current drug regime has such difficulty getting through, it is unlikely that the nuances of social background, which the G. P. does understand, will get across the invisible barrier at the hospital front gates. And the G. P. who, unsurprisingly, fails to attend a social work conference at 11 o'clock on Monday morning is disdainfully written off as part of the problem.

As for the patients, they show an infinite patience and unfortunate ability to put up with what they get, peppered with occasional outbursts and the odd complaint which more often concerns speculation about the doctor's love-life than his diagnostic limitations. G. P.s cultivate either a democratic manner and a comforting but indiscriminate largesse or a mildly belligerent approach to all but the most seriously ill patient. And both approaches result from a recognition that some mask or other is a necessary defence from behind which to scrutinise a very mixed succession of needs only a limited proportion of which can be given any genuine help. As for the rest, general practice is a business which I once heard a consultant chirpily call 'highly skilled reassurance'. I am sure he meant it as a compliment but it expressed exactly the limitations with which most primary care is struggling along.

The teaching of general practice in medical schools has grown from next to nothing to become the subject of specialised university departments. But even the best textbooks and medical schools cannot prepare you for the sheer variety of demands and sorts of trust patients want. Hospital teaching is based on uncommon but interesting disease demonstrated by all-knowing consultants and the mastery of an immense body of scientific fact. Yet however sophisticated the newly qualified doctor is in dealing with computerised quizzes, he or she is a novice in the maze of hunches, background information, social insights and medical suspicion through which a good G. P. has learnt to find a way. Safe inside a hospital, the junior doctor can afford to be cocky, protected by a white coat, backed up by a small army of unacknowledged underlings, bolstered by the proximity of senior colleagues. But in the firing-line of primary medicine, as you urgently scrawl scripts with a packed waiting-room coughing accusingly at every question, it is hard not to feel you are failing to sustain the scientific standards hallowed at medical school.

More and more, what start as strictly medical questions go beyond medicine itself. Many common problems of tension, over-eating, addictions of various sorts, have their roots in how people live and work. To tackle them with pills alone may seem scientific, but it in fact violates the deeper canons of serious medicine. Many of the questions patients now ask do not require a simple 'yes' or 'no', backed by some magnificent but unexplained authority; they require the doctor to present information so that the patient can make the decision.

What are the risks inherent in the hospitalisation of older patients and how do they compare with the disadvantages of home care? Is the use of new and energetically promoted preparations (say, to ease the menopause by hormone therapy, or to increase blood flow to the brains of the elderly) justified? What are patients' rights over their own bodies – especially when, as in the case of abortion, the patient's wishes conflict with medical and religious established wisdom?

These questions, and others like them, once had a simple answer: the doctor was a 'God with a bedside manner.' Part of his informal training was learning the skill of telling convincing lies and over-whelming difficult enquiries with a blast of long medical words or a brief bit of soothing.

As long as the patient could be seen as a simpleton who happened to be accompanying his body, the doctor had a vested interest in maintaining his patient's ignorance. There was more stress on fitting in socially with senior colleagues than on being able to talk openly and clearly to people who happened to be sick; and in fact many patients wanted to cling to this almost religious but very comforting role. As regards their own diagnosis, treatment and anatomy, ignorance *was* bliss.

But now, for most doctors and most patients, this era of medical infallibility is over. Most newly qualified doctors, at last educated more widely in sociology and psychiatry and drawn from a wider class background, start in practice aiming at an honest, democratic relationship with their patients based on the skills they do possess rather than on mysterious powers of social authority. They appreciate rather than disdain the 'lay' knowledge of their patients. There is a commitment to screening and prevention and a determination to apply a scientific approach rather than simply to regurgitate it. Primary care *is* better organised, better financed, better informed, better paid and potentially strengthened by the shift of emphasis towards community care.

However, a G. P.'s ability to serve his patients is still defined by the public's traditional ideas of doctoring and by the material circumstances in which he works. The average size of the G. P.'s list has not been reduced significantly and in working-class areas dependence on migrant doctors has increased. Patients still wait too long and are seen too briefly.

A Suffolk G. P. replied to criticism of over-officious practice secretaries: 'The answer lies in providing better health education to enable people to recognise and treat mild self-limiting illness and in recruiting more GPs so that the average NHS list is reduced.' The B. M. A. made a similarly practical reply to the Parliamentary Commission on wife-beating which wrote scathingly that 'It is not enough for doctors just to treat physical injuries and dispense tranquillisers.' The B. M. A. retorted, with some justice: 'It is no good slanging family doctors when there are not adequate social services available in many areas to which GPs can refer such patients.'

A new general practitioner

G. P.s are only human. They are under very considerable direct pressure from the drug companies. The G. P. is the middle-man between them and their market; each one prescribes, on average, over £14,000 worth of drugs a year. There is not only direct sales contact to pamper personally the last of such big spenders but sponsorship of give-away medical publications which mix academic medicine with wine know-how, stock-market tips and hard-sell advertisements. Pity not only the G. P. but the G. P.'s postman also. Practitioners themselves have become responsible for a great deal of administrative and clerical work. They are facing, in the cuts, the shrinking of the very services which were promised as an essential part of a new deal for primary care. The fact that a Ministry computer has come to the decision, on economic grounds, that a local hospital must be closed or group-practice building postponed yet again does not make it a decision which is medically sound.

The G. P.'s traditional role has been undermined, and yet nothing more tangible seems about to replace it. Many doctors are in a quandary: on the one hand, they genuinely want more medical team work and a better-educated public; on the other, they are reluctant to relinquish their old authority and unique responsibility. G. P.s are, in this respect, victims of their own reputation of omniscience. They are still expected to have influence over the housing authorities and the law courts who, nowadays, disregard their carefully penned pleas. And they are still expected to deal with medical and social crises long after the social workers have packed up office. I have found it sobering to see how often the G. P. and the police officer, targets of so much radical social criticism, end up doling out the common humanity that Family Crisis Intervention Units and community activists accuse them of lacking. Indeed, read carefully, the current complaints of the police and the general practitioners are quite radical in their implications: they are saying they can no longer cope with the degree of social unrest that becomes their responsibility; that they resent their work becoming a substitute for political change; that they want to return to chasing criminals and healing the sick instead of providing a complaints bureau for a disgruntled and divided society.

Indeed for city doctors this problem is worsening. The era of 'community care', by coinciding with the epoch of 'the cuts', has turned out as somewhat of a confidence trick. The traditional support of hospitals is becoming more partial and hard to obtain, while the expansion of community-based facilities, the necessary counterbalance to any hospital closure, is proving elusive. Many essential and long-promised community facilities, in particular day-care centres for the old and sheltered dwelling for the newly discharged psychiatric patient, are shelved and the services are operated at such a level of chronic understaffing that only emergencies are tackled and then often with reluctance. Especially in mental health, the old set-up has been abolished and the new, born into a financial vacuum, is in disarray. And it is the G. P. who is expected, by the relatives at least, to carry the can, just as in the family the mother is once again expected to act as amateur nurse, psychiatrist, ward orderly and therapist as well as carry out her usual domestic work, and often a job into the bargain. Department of Health promises have proved as inflated as the Treasury's currency; a 70-year-old lady with heart trouble, sent home with an aluminium walking-frame, and a tray of council-cooked carbohydrates pushed through her door four times a week by a 'meals-on-wheels' lady who would love to talk but 'Just hasn't got the time', confided that she thought she would have been better looked after in the 1930s: 'At least you didn't have to be dying to be let into hospital in them days', she told me.

It is these kinds of pressure, the sense of being permanently under seige and the shrinking of real resources which give rise to the popularity of the answering services, whose real effect is to funnel most requests into day-time hours. Those who have seized on these services as a symbol of the indolence of the general practitioner are attacking a symptom, not the cause. And they might reflect, as the night-visiting doctor often does, that the claim for night calls stands at about one-quarter of that charged by night plumbers, and that in urban America home visits are almost unheard of at any time of the day. In the absence of genuine health centres, emergency services are inevitable; they should be accepted and run by the Family Practitioner Committees themselves rather than commercial firms.

What's going wrong?

A key to change in general practice is lay criticism. Julian Tudor Hart, of the Glyncorrwg Health Centre in Glamorgan, is one of the radical G. P.s who argue that the new primary-care doctor must be exposed to open criticism by medical peers and by patients and operate in a genuinely democratic team. This process would depend on the participation of a much more active, knowledgeable public. He says that 'The most evangelistic of health promotion and anticipatory care cannot be effective if the mass of people have a fatalistic approach to their own health.'

David Ryde, a South London G. P. and member of the Royal College of General Practitioners, has recently described how his own illness forced him to think carefully about traditional reliance on pills and ignorance, and inclined him towards the idea of the doctor as 'a purveyor of ideas, an interpreter and an educationalist in health'. His drug prescriptions now amount to only a third of the national average prescribed by G. P.s. He feels that 'a doctor's prescribing costs are inversely related to his grasp of the problem and his understanding of the patient, and to achieve this, the doctor must listen. The doctor who looks at his watch instead of his patient should take a long look at himself.'

Here again the most influential criticism of medical mystery-mongering has come from the Women's Liberation Movement, in the form of their demands for health care which starts from the patient's absolute right over his own body. Professor Peter Huntingford, a London obstetrician, has argued positively that this kind of challenge is not a nuisance but an inspiration to doctors who really want to practise medicine which starts from the real needs of the patients and not from the convenience of the doctor. 'I have been forced,' he has said, 'to question my own attitudes because I was fortunate enough to be involved with a group of consumers who have questioned the attitudes of myself and others like me who wished to care for them.' In this field, doctors will find study of *Spare Rib*'s medical pages and feminist self-help manuals more challenging and illuminating than their professional journals.

Perhaps it is only when other sections of the community have the confidence to want control over their bodies too that medical professionalism will back down. For that confidence to develop, the maximum of well-informed lay debate is desirable, even if it does dent doctors' self-esteem. To assert more control over the medical institutions they pay for, the lay public needs the knowledge to challenge medical secrecy on informed terms. Medicine is much too important to be left to doctors alone.

5
Mental health

Madness is no longer taboo; but it is talked about in a special tone as something that happens to someone else. Mr Normal, Mrs Normal and Baby Normal smile graciously at the camera and make quite sure that each other's facade is straight. But as any G. P. knows, Mr Normal is a drunk, his wife is on valium and the baby has to wet the bed to attract their attention. The normality of family life is a carefully achieved invention. The neighbours might believe it but doctors do not. Five million people consult them each year about mental-health problems, and 30 million working days were lost in 1976 because of mental and emotional problems (ten times the number caused by strikes) and one in six of us, higher in the case of doctors, can expect to spend some time as a mental-hospital patient. Over 80,000 school-age children are emotionally disturbed enough to need professional help, while two in a hundred people are mentally handicapped. We all know someone who has been or will be mentally ill. It might well be ourselves.

Yet until recently mental treatment seemed designed according to the precept 'out of sight, out of mind.' Patients were either given pills and left to work their own way through the turmoil of their fears, tears and desperation, or they were exiled in distant, overcrowded asylums. A third of all people in hospital are mental patients but only a tenth of our doctors and a fifth of our nurses are available to attend to them. One hospital in seven still has no psychologist and less than half the psychiatric nurses are qualified. Until twenty years ago no one even seemed to care about this terrifying state of affairs. Now it is a suitable subject for concern. But very little gets done and in many ways the plight of the mentally ill is worsening again.

The problem of reform without resources is illustrated most strikingly in mental health, where the movement towards community psychiatry and the ending of the anti-therapeutic and increasingly expensive asylum system has landed more and more patients with the worst of both worlds, without the protection of hospital and with very sketchy and threadbare support outside it.

Victorian psychiatry

Despite previous eras of reform, often reflecting a radical upsurge in society, at the beginning of this century therapeutic gloom still confined the majority of mental patients to remote asylums where they were imprisoned at low cost. Since treatment was non-existent and madness thought hereditary, the vigorous prevention of sexual intercourse was the main aim of doctors, isolated within their own profession and suspected by the public. Growing interest in possible organic causes led to a few doctors of a biological training accumulating much descriptive information, but these systems of classification were not the basis of active treatment until the discovery of biochemical and physical methods. Psychoanalysis unlocked the key to the neuroses and was an active treatment method *par excellence*, but, for practical as well as political reasons, has, tragically, never made real inroads into British psychiatry and society.

The early treatment methods were as pragmatic as they were barbaric. Wagner-Jauregg injected bacteria to cause an artificial fever in Vienna in the hope that, through the haze of nightmarish pyrexia, sanity might stalk back. The discovery of insulin coma (by Sakel in Hungary), of electro-shock (by Cerletta in Italy), of leucotomy (by Moniz in Portugal) and most importantly the synthesis of the major tranquillisers did offer an alternative to purely custodial methods.

Institutional neurosis

A post-war group of American sociologists and British psychiatrists developed independently an analysis suggesting that at least part of the disturbance of the patients undergoing long-term asylum treatment as part of the functioning of the very institution. The mental hospital operated an intricate system of social control within which a new patient ascended or descended through wards informally graded by allowable misconduct, at the mercy of the considerable power of the nurse to punish or give privileges, as long as a psychiatric reason was given. But it would only be a reason, for while the diagnosis may have been medical, the treatment very seldom was. When patients were most willing to improve their social contact, they were most likely to be brought to the attention of a doctor as deserving attention, so that the patient who needed help most was least likely to receive it. Ward conferences were held without regard to patients' real needs, the effort being instead directed to agreeing on a diagnostic label. This exploration of the sociology of the cuckoo's nest and the attitudes of the doctors also explained the inevitable failure of the recurring cycle of *exposé*, reform and then apathy.

About the same time the population of British medical hospitals had reached a point of such overcrowding that 'treatment is handicapped, the hospital atmosphere is disrupted and patient attitudes are adversely affected', according to the consultants themselves.[1] The practical pressures reinforced the theoretical points made by the reformers. In fact, the realities behind the ornate mullions and spacious but always empty lawns and parks were even worse than the psychiatrists dare admit. Patients had by and large surrendered to the rules of the institution, lacking even the rudimentary possessions with which to assemble an identity. Rehabilitation was designed with the economic efficiency of the hospital as its first concern. Staff were distant, hidden behind their roles and were quite often unstable as well. Routine use of sedatives and major transquillisers, demoralising ward atmosphere and the concentration of medical effort on only a couple of wards left the rest of the backward patients at the mercy of the nurses. Rees at Warlingham described the pyramid of power: 'The ordinary nurses had a key that could single-lock any door. The junior doctors and the sisters had keys which could double-lock patients and nurses in wards, and with my master key I could go round and lock the whole lot of them in.'[2]

The permanent tremors, social withdrawal, flatness of effect, lack of speech and endless repetition of single phrases and movements shared by the faded figures who edged down corridors as if they were precipices or argued with themselves in a ward corner chair were in part products of the hospital regime, acquired long after the original cause for admission had disappeared. Contact from 'outside' was closed off completely; across the park was another world. If they could not get out within the first year they were there for life. Even in 1977, 30,000 people have been in mental hospital for twenty years or more. As a student I worked in a unit attempting to ease long-stay patients back into shared, sheltered dwellings in the towns they had grown up in. I had to visit relatives to sound them out about the possibility of their loved ones leaving hospital. One old lady had been in the hospital thirty-two years and her sister told me the only reason she ever went in was because she had 'a breakdown' in the church when her betrothed jilted her. Yet when we mentioned the possibility of her returning home, her family's faces fell in collective horror and they fell over each other with excuses about why they could not have anything to do with the process. In the 1950s asylums were about as easy to leave as dungeons.

Nevertheless, the combination of the use of drugs with skilled rehabilitation methods pressed ahead in an attempt to develop rather than destroy what remained positive in the patient and support it with what resources could be mobilised among relatives, the community and 'half-way' institutions. Although the effort started with the oldest institutionalised patients, it implied new methods to prevent the same cycle getting a grip on new patients. Pioneer work at Henderson, Dingleton and Shenley used the ideas of the therapeutic community which had originated in the treatment of young, largely male patients suffering from war neuroses to alter and democratise hospital in-patient life. Instead of mentally rotting while waiting for an occasional interview with a doctor, the other twenty-three hours of the day, with other relationships with fellow patients and the nursing staff who were permanently on the ward, were seen as a valuable part of therapy in its own right. The psychiatric and political implications of this approach were developed most fully by Ronald Laing and David Cooper in that dazzling burst of British 'anti-psychiatry'. Although both have turned into gurus and have since produced enigmatic collections of epigrams for the troubled middle classes, their formative and most interesting work was done with working-class patients in National Health Service hospitals.

Subnormality

The case was even stronger in the subnormality service, which accounted for half of the patients receiving local-authority funds: 50,000 mentally handicapped people still live in hospital, 6000 of them children. The 'colonies' or long-stay institutions for the defective assumed that improvement or useful treatment was not possible and what remained was custodial care undertaken with various degrees of humanity; But mental handicap is not an illness, but a permanent disability which can be helped by education and training. Closer study by a Medical Research Council unit has shown that although the severely subnormal, usually suffering from clear-cut brain pathology or Down's syndrome, tend to improve little and to be bedfast and incontinent, many of the less severely subnormal children suffer from a more temporary incapacity and are able to make dramatic improvements if they get positive treatment instead of the barrack ward. Inflexible, regimented treatment, depersonalisation, especially lack of possessions and clothes, the social distance of the staff, indicated by uniforms, separate canteens, a dislike of physical contact and a tendency to give orders instead of just talking, all characteristic of the older, poorly staffed hospitals, were the worst possible treatment. Migrant children, particularly West Indians, suffer especially in this kind of home, to which they are more often sent than their white equivalents.

On arrival at a newer style of home, the subnormal children at first reacted to their new freedom with frightening, inexplicable tantrums where anger and grief mingled with bewilderment at the abrupt lack of punishment and restraint. The longer they had been in institutional care, the more painful was their arrival:

'very often a child would fly into uncontrollable storms of anger and grief in which he would beat his head against a wall or bite an arm hard enough to draw blood' [but after two years there was a marked improvement in mental age and, more importantly] 'the old pathological behaviour had largely gone, nearly all the children were able to enjoy simple group play with other children for long periods, they talked quite a lot among themselves and they are affectionate and happy children, usually busy and interested in what they are doing.[3]

The National Association for Mental Health (MIND) estimates that 35,000 more places are needed in occupation and training centres than are now available. As things are, the majority of subnormal children will simply never get the chance to discover their own human potential. Instead they will be made more subnormal by a process of victimisation so routine it is hard to perceive.

The 1961 hospital plan

On the basis of this early evidence, as well as the annual prodding of the ever-mounting costs of the Victorian asylums, built like the railways of the same era – to last – a plan of closures was announced in 1961 which forecast that 'the acute population of mental hospitals was to drop by half in the next ten years and the long term population was ultimately to dwindle to zero'. In its place was to be a new era of co-operation between local-authority services and psychiatrists based in mental wards of the new district general hospitals, united in an attempt to prevent chronicity and to treat most patients in their homes or in their local areas. Tooth and Brookes's famous curve which showed the entire long-stay population of mental hospitals disappearing completely by 1975, through death or discharge, and a much lower ratio of beds (1.8 per 1000 rather than 3.3), was uncritically incorporated into the plan.

In practice, only one half of the bargain was kept. There was a forced decline in the number of hospital beds; but there was also a very slow and uneven provision of the local-authority services on which patients were now to rely, a further decline in morale and conditions for the patients and doctors stranded by the run-down and a very slow development of district general hospital wards, which consequently came under very heavy pressure. After the initial burst of success with rehabilitation of dischargeable chronics, a more intractable and unresponsive group were revealed, most of whom now had no personal contact whatsoever with the outside world. The rate of admission, far from falling away from the 1959 level, increased by 30 per cent and epidemiological studies showed a frightening degree of undisclosed and untreated serious psychiatric illness. A field study in Anglesey unearthed 1104 ill patients who had never seen a psychiatrist, including forty-five schizophrenics and forty-eight sufferers of organic mental illness. A similar study of G.P.s showed that, although 14 per cent of their consultations are on purely psychiatric grounds, only three in a hundred of their patients were referred to psychiatrists. The rate of re-admission for those who went to hospital also stayed high.[4] For many the open door turned out to be the revolving door.

Community care?

Not only was the tempo of building pitifully slow, reflecting the low prestige the mental health service still had, but the quality of many of the facilities was poor and tended towards the very institutionalisation they attempted to avert. For every futurist general-hospital psychiatric ward with armchairs and original acrylic paintings, there were inactive day centres, authoritarian hostels and unvisited sitting-rooms. The mounting difficulties for anyone, let alone someone emerging painfully from hospital treatment, to find a home and a job, prevented the final critical step of re-entry into normal life. Although families did their best to support ex-patients against the odds of low income, overcrowded homes and their own poor health, there was often evidence that the mental health of the patients and the relatives got worse rather than better.

A survey of the hostel accommodation with professedly re-habilitation aims found that 60 per cent were less permissive than the hospital wards themselves and some were staffed by people who had left the hospital service in protest against relaxation of disciplinarian methods! The day hospitals too, usually in old Victorian houses in residential areas rather than being custom-built, increased their patients fourfold in the 1960s but provided little more than social supervision, acting more as a long-stay day ward for chronic patients whose illness had stabilised, and apart from some rather arbitrary E. C. T. provided little active treatment.

Industrial therapy, once the corner-stone of rehabilitation, proved less than triumphant. In one of the best centres at Bristol, after seven years and 678 patients, only 174 were established in open employment. In many schemes, the industrial work provided is simply used to give chronic patients 'something to do', has no therapeutic value and is very badly paid into the bargain. The slow development of group and health-centre practices has slowed the G. P.s' involvement in community care. Instead of co-ordinating clinical and social services, the G. P. is indifferent to both and tends to treat minor psychiatric illnesses with enormous and ever-growing quantities of commercial tranquillisers. There is relatively little evidence of awareness of how changes in the care of the mentally ill will alter the future role of the G. P.

Crisis psychiatry

The danger of being confined and forgotten in a mental hospital which quickly reduced its inhabitants to a uniform level of incompetence by coercive wholesale rulings is gone. The local authorities have a duty to re-integrate rather than a power to apprehend. The quality of psychiatric social work has improved out of recognition. But a new set of dangers now prevails. This movement was a child of economic necessity. 'Finance is still the best crude criteria of our commitment to community care', states Titmuss, and judged on that basis the authorities care very little. All the faults of the asylums can be reproduced in community settings. Instead of a fear of permanent unwilling admission, there is now worry about regaining admission when it is needed desparately, so hard-pressed are the existing psychiatric beds. If psychiatrists were over-anxious to admit once, nowadays in-patient mental care is often hard to get, discharge is early, and appointments, even for emergencies, long in the future.

The community has proved a singularly inhospitable place. In central London one now sees more openly demented people on the street than I remember ten years ago. A jab of depot tranquilliser, a short course of E. C. T. and an appointment three months hence with a note to the G. P. can sometimes be as uncaring as the back wards of the asylums. Those who can survive with the good offices and pills of the G. P. are fortunate for, lacking resources, the humanitarian slogan of community psychiatry can turn out to be a cruel joke.

6
The drug industry

Profiteering, price-fixing, promotion of ineffective and dangerous goods, questionable advertising, high-pressure sales techniques, suppression of information, ferocious rivalry leading to monopoly trading – it sounds like Chicago in the era of Prohibition. It describes the painstakingly documented growth of the pharmaceuticals industry whose business is not illegal hooch but life-saving chemistry. It is ironic that the industry with the most honourable of purposes, the relief of suffering, exhibits the most piratical features of modern big business. Starting from the anguish of patients dabbing their tears in a busy surgery, through shelves burdened with unread and unreadable research, to glistening laboratories, and ending in company headquarters in three continents (all done with the secrecy of the C. I. A.), the giant companies have woven a world of their own. They are perhaps the classic example of the bad habits of big business, the lack of scruple engendered by the profit motive and the literal irresponsibility of the modern multinational.

Drugs, not very long ago dispensed from common ingredients in a backroom of the surgery, have become the biggest of big business, whose vastness cannot be grasped and whose power is such that it can render the N. H. S., in theory a monopoly purchaser, pathetically vulnerable, can defy Royal Commissions and laugh in the face of attempts to reform it. An industry that more than any other has a responsibility to those who consume its products perverts their real needs. The companies' influence is no longer merely financial. They do much to mould research, therapy, education and the whole ethos of contemporary medicine. Their growth and their still unchecked power is the most dramatic example of how the idealism of the N. H. S. has been exploited by commercial interests and how doctors' insistence on their professional freedoms – in this case the freedom to

prescribe – has instead meant their dependence on commercial firms'
definitions and the reversal of Parcelius's honourable maxim, 'I seek
not to enrich the apothecaries, but to cure the sick.'

Put simply, there are now too many drugs produced. They are
overpriced and promoted misleadingly. Their overconsumption is
itself a major cause of illness, their overprescription a substitute for
clinical skill, and their overpricing a crucial cause of the poverty of
the N. H. S. In our profligate use of prescribed drugs as well as
addictives and chemist-shop remedies, we are squandering precious
medical resources and generating unnecessary risks in a way which
will shock succeeding generations in the way the Victorian sewers
now turn us aghast. Mood-altering drugs, prescribed by mainly male,
always middle-class doctors as a substitute for altering the conditions
which give rise to depression, sleeplessness, unhappiness, increase the
mainly female, mainly working-class women's sense of passivity and
self-reproach. They try to enforce a chemical solution on what is
more often a social or sexual, and therefore a political, problem. And
we inflict a system which is a scandal in the industrialised West on the
poor world where it is nothing less than a crime. East and West, it
locks the doctor and the patient in a false relationship where both are
obliged to pretend that swallowing pills will solve health, and other,
problems. Yet attempts to reform the system bounce off ineffectively
against the protective exteriors of the companies.

Origins

How has this situation arisen so rapidly? The major discoveries in
organic chemistry and immunology were in the nineteenth century
but large-scale pharmacology had to await the expansion of the
chemical and oil-related industries during the First and Second
World Wars respectively for their crucial leaps in scale. War was once
again the bloody midwife of medical innovation and the pharmaceuticals industry emerged, no longer as purveyors of laxative pills
and tonics with the inventor's bewhiskered profile on the bottle, but
as a major chemical industry in its own right. Over the ten years
before 1972, the British industry expanded at an annual rate of 10 per
cent, a good three times the rate of manufacturing industry. The
world industry has expanded faster. Britain is the seventh largest
consumer, although the most successful British manufacturer is
sixteenth in the league of producers and only four British companies
are in the top forty.

A year after the N. H. S. began, Britain's drug bill was £39m.; in 1974 it had risen to £327m. The cost of the pharmaceutical services as a percentage of the total cost of the N. H. S. moved from 8.4 per cent in 1950 to 10.1 per cent in 1969. From 1972 to 1974 the growth rate of the hospital drugs bill was greater than the growth rate for any other sector. According to the D. H. S. S. consultative document *Priorities for Health and Personal Services in England* the pharmaceutical services accounted for 43 per cent of the total cost of the primary-care services in 1975–6, and this percentage was projected to increase during the succeeding five years.[1] This remorseless growth in drug purchase does not, unfortunately, represent genuine therapeutic breakthroughs – there have been few – but the ramification of remedies of comparable properties but differing packaging, and higher price tags.

As viewed by the potential investor, pharmaceutical shares offer a return on capital even higher than that promised by the frozen-food and soft-drink industries but with the added virtue of morally legitimate aims. Small wonder competition within this exceptionally lucrative market is so bloodthirsty. The industry has become highly centralised and has seen a high-tempo sequence of mergers and takeovers in the 1960s which mopped up most of the smaller companies and transformed the bigger national companies into multinational giants. In Britain today, five companies control approximately 30 per cent of the market. Three Swiss firms control 15 per cent of world sales. And the process is accelerating as all serious competition, except by equivalent-sized giants, is reduced to scavenging at the droppings from the top tables.

The laws of patent and the tendency for the big companies to divide up the pill market render 'market forces', always rather fictional, quite moribund, and free competition a delusion. Real profit levels, especially of the Swiss-based companies, are guarded jealously. A former Roche employee who revealed details of Roche's contracts for vitamins was jailed for industrial espionage. The return on capital employed is often as high as 70 per cent and declared profit levels in the big British firms, Boots and Beechams, were 45 per cent and 41 per cent respectively in 1972, while in the United States the second biggest firm, Merck, Sharp and Dohme, netted 50 per cent. The profit levels extracted from the less-developed countries are equally high. In India the thirty-three foreign-controlled drug firms, supplying 65 per cent – 75 per cent of the total market showed average profits of 30 per cent in 1970. A confidential World Health Authority Report found that whereas Britain pays $2.40 per kilo for vitamin C, India has to pay nearly $10 per kilo. A quantity of tetracycline antibiotics, which would cost $24–$30 in Europe, is sold to India, Pakistan and Columbia for between $100 and $270. The absence of either genuine market competition or effective enforcement of machinery for price controls means that there is an inbuilt tendency to overprice. This, and the grotesque profit levels, are justified by the costs of research and development which the drug companies claim are uniquely high and involve undue risk. Although the avarice of many of the most ethical suppliers has been for some time masked by the 'transfer pricing mechanism', a device whereby a subsidiary processes ingredients which it then 'sells' to the parent at greatly inflated cost – which the manufacturing stage of the operation (often not a great deal more than the putting of goods into capsules) further increases.

Research

Undoubtedly the fundamental research, following blind hunches but necessary for real innovation, *is* expensive and so too is the very methodical and exhaustive safety testing of new drugs which ought, but does not always, precede their mass marketing. But the apparently impressive resources devoted to research need to be looked at on a comparative basis. On average research and development expenditure comprises only 10 per cent of costs while advertising and promotion take up nearly 20 per cent. The industry's contribution to total medical research has fallen over ten years from about a third to nearly a quarter of the total budget. The drug companies' research bill included trivial investigations of acceptability of package colour and prestige conference expenses, 'me-too' investigations into subtle alterations of rival formulations to get round patent laws, and simply money squandered in the early stages of drugs, only 1 in 5000 of which will reach the market. Such is the investment placed on the back of that one successful product, that, once launched, research thereafter must be favourable. However *bona fide* its financing and scientific pedigree, it becomes a species of advertising, shaded paragraphs of which will be flashed under doctors' noses in the course of a sales talk, between the embossed desk-pad and the free samples.

It is certainly clear that commercial research has not prevented the steady increase of drug interactions and death and illness from prescribed medicines. In 1974 in England and Wales, 549 people died as a result of a drug overdose and therapeutic misadventures.

Adverse reactions to medicines account for 5 per cent of the admissions to hospital medical wards, and between 10 per cent and 15 per cent of patients suffer an adverse reaction of one type or another during their admission. There is a growing list of disease syndromes which are known to be the legacy of a previous generation of physicians over-enthusiastically prescribing oral steroids, in particular harvesting a large net of unexpected complications from long-term therapy. Even such commonplace medicines as the 'white medicine' for gastric acidity can affect the performance of other drugs taken simultaneously.

When drug side-effects have been discovered, there is little in doctors' or manufacturers' behaviour so far to justify great confidence. The Distillers Company did their level best to avoid paying adequate compensation to the limbless victims of thalidomide; and that Eraldin induced eye damage came to light through a letter to a medical journal rather than the formal 'yellow card' early-warning system, although subsequent to that report some 200 cases were notified retrospectively. But a full twelve months after the drug was withdrawn, in July 1975, patients were still receiving it. Most doctors simply assume that only safe drugs are marketed. Most manufacturers take safety seriously but within the over-all framework of aggressive 'safemanship'. In one letter I received recently there was a warning about the hazards of tricyclic anti-depressant overdosage, but it turned out to be from the marketing director of a firm producing a rival tetracyclic preparation!

Although it is fashionable to be 'in research', the worth of a lot of it, in more fields than the medical, seems questionable and needs to be firmly measured against existing need. Research into ways of making more money or making people consume more is downright harmful. So is the overbalancing of research resources so markedly towards pharmeuticals when we know so little about more fundamental factors such as our patients' diets, the effects of different physical treatments and the identification of pollution and health hazards. It serves once again to distort, almost without us noticing it, the nature of illness, turning it into a sort of commodity which can only be dealt with by another, rival, commodity. It is absurd that sheaves of sound, if repetitive, material is on hand about the effect of a chest inhaler on lung volume but it is impossible to measure or assay the composition of the air that patient will breathe into his newly expanded lungs in the fume-choked streets outside the surgery window. Nor is the research target disinterested. Attempts to undertake the elementary step of independently testing the efficacy of drugs are considered highly unsuitable research by the industry, which itself estimates the N. H. S. pays £15 million a year for useless preparations. In 1965 a panel of British experts assessing the therapeutic effectiveness of 2241 of the 3000 products then available, judged 35 per cent of them ineffective, obsolete or irrational combinations, and in 1971 a similar investigation of 2000 products by a panel of the American Food and Drug Administration (F. D. A.) found that 60 per cent lacked evidence for their therapeutic claims. It is now well recognised that up to 50 per cent of patients do not take their drugs as prescribed, a syndrome known as 'poor treatment adherence', which not only lowers the beneficial effect of treatment but wastes money and stockpiles unwanted but potentially dangerous drugs. But why should the companies worry if patients do not keep taking the medicine? Their business is to sell it.

In Britain the drug industry managed to close down *Proplist*, an independent pharmacopoeia, which listed some preparations as frankly ineffective, and the excellent but tiny *Prescriber's Journal*, a mine of sensible therapeutics, produced by clinical experts, is buried under the volume of commercial drug mail.

Product testing

Further, not all research is as scrupulous as it should be. Particularly in North America there is evidence that poor, coloured or desperate subjects were used as guinea-pigs in tests where risks were very great. The women of Puerto Rico were selected as a suitable and docile control group for the first testing of the birth-control pill before it was used in the United States. During this period the Puerto Ricans were 'tried out' on doses both lower and higher than the effective amount. Likewise, long-stay prisoners have been tempted with remission of sentence in exchange for volunteering for high-risk drug experiments. The C. I. A. are known to have tested psychedelic drugs on unknowing victims. Perhaps in some cases the researchers are not as malicious as it might seem, but it does point to a gigantic double-standard.

This lack of scruple has also been apparent in the recent chemical-plant disasters. The Seveso explosion in July 1976 hurled the contents of a reactor containing dioxin, a chemical by-product hard to degrade and extremely dangerous even in small doses, in a poison cloud over many acres. It was several days before Roche, the responsible company, undertook proper analysis. In that time the poison spread, crops wilted, dogs died and unborn children were deformed in the womb. The full toll is still unknown. Similar tragedies in Amsterdam, at Flixborough and the Coalite works in Bolsover suggest that the chemical giants are not prepared to spend the required money on safety or do sufficiently frank research on production and waste-product risks until it is too late.

It is also inevitable that drug companies are reluctant to undertake commercial research into rare disease where there is no prospect of general application and, hence, high returns. Nor is much attention paid to the widespread illness in areas and among people too poor to make the grade as potential purchasers. Indeed only 1 per cent of the total spent by industry, governments and charity on medical research is devoted to the major disease problems of the developing world. There is little interest in natural as opposed to petrochemical sources, although, for example, Chinese experts have identified some 500 species of plant growing in Tanzania, extracts of which are in current use in Chinese medical practice. It is surely lack of confidence in modern commercial medicines which is leading to a revival in this country of interest in traditional and folk remedies which, even if not particularly successful, do not do harm to the patient.

Promotion

If research costs are inflated, promotional expenses are grotesque. Not only is the relative budget higher than even the soft-soap industry but it is focused on only 56,000 doctors who in 1972 had over £570 spent on each of them, including over a hundredweight of literature and gifts. The biggest item is paying for representatives, often trained scientifically, some 3000 of whom, one for every five doctors, lurk in hospital canteens and wait in doctor's queues in order to visit doctors. At present rates the average doctor can expect to have £30,000 spent on his 'education' by the drug companies, about twice the cost of the real thing at medical school. The drug companies provide the most insistent form of postgraduate education most G. P.s receive.

It is of course the drugs of dubious merit which require the most lavish promotion. The treatments for diabetes are standard and of proven value so the manufacturing companies only need to spend 1.9 per cent of the total cost of the drug on advertising. For antacids and cough and cold remedies whose real clinical value is dubious but for which the potential market is immense, the amount spent on advertising is 13.9 per cent and 12.9 per cent respectively.

Another worrying factor is the degree to which drug companies have direct links with medical faculties. In the *Lancet* one consultant wrote: 'very few in our profession and practically none of the general public realise that some of the holders of professional chairs and important positions in the medical world also act as paid advisors to industrial concerns. This may not affect their judgement, but they may reasonably be asked to declare their interests.'[2]

The quality of material has improved somewhat but the removal of the worst excesses has only shown how bad the remaining features are. The absurdly glossy and overwritten free magazines, bulging with advice on tax evasion and vintage motoring, the heavy lunches preceded by a perfunctory snippet of film, the three-dimensional diagrams which are unfolded in a carefully rehearsed sales pitch, with the stumbled chemical names and the innuendos about the gullibility of patients, reflect as badly on a profession which succumbs to such perfidious flattery as they do on an industry which practises them. It is a mockery of the years of training in organic chemistry and the inculcation of meticulous habits of observation that one should end up leafing through the trade gazette of drugs, *MIMS*, head reeling with the fancified trade names devised for items only differing in the degree of overpricing, no longer able to recall the dosage of the basic treatment taught at medical school. We prescribe under a bombardment of brand-named calendars, stencilled biros, embossed tongue depressers, and sexiest advertising, rather lower in its standards than that used to promote after-shave lotion. It positively encourages doctors to avoid tackling factors like industrial pollution, smoking, diet, stress, lack of exercise, excessive alcohol intake and way-of-life factors in illness, and instead binds us to the chariot of the latest chemical innovation whose impetus might be medical but whose final motive will be commercial.

This rampant commercialism is particularly objectionable when it is directed towards problems which are themselves products of the competitive, profit motivated system. The state of being overweight and the need for slimming are direct results of a society which eats too much badly processed, unhealthy food and which, at the same time, places abnormal stress on physical appearance as the supreme index of social worth.

The slimming business has now wrung an £80m. market out of people's unhappiness, half of which is spent on dietory breads and crispbreads, the rest on a medley of inflatable belts, massage soaps, muscle-exercise machines and other profitable nonsense. The plain truth is that only diet and exercise will reduce excess fat, but neither make money. Some of the larger dietary bread manufacturers are subsidiaries of the very processing giants whose instant-food products are tasteless, unhealthy, fattening and play their part i creating obesity. Even when doctors point out that the low bulk volume of processed food is a probable cause of constipation, diverticular disease, the irritable bowel syndrome and possibly bowel cancer, a queue of firms marketing artificial bulk expanders and bran products forms promptly.

The most offensive case of making profits out of unhappiness is in the field of the minor tranquillisers. In financial terms, the N. H. S. was subjected to what amounts to daylight robbery, although no one is impolite enough to use those terms. The Monopoly Commission Report shows conclusively that Roche netted £24m. from sales in Britain alone in the period 1966–72 by selling the drug ingredients to a subsidiary at vastly inflated prices which bear no resemblance to real costs.[3] By this means real profits were safely siphoned away to the parent company and discreetly buried in inaccessible accounts. In 1970, Roche Products (U. K.) was purchasing the ingredients for Librium and Valium at £370 and £922 per kilo respectively from the parent in Switzerland when the same ingredients could be bought for £9 and £20 per kilo respectively in Italy. The Commission modestly calculated that the real profits to the company on sales of Librium and Valium were 55 per cent and 60 per cent respectively, implying a return on capital employed of over 70 per cent. Meanwhile in Colombia the overpricing on Valium was 6.155 per cent and on Librium 6.478 per cent. At the height of their patent life, the two drugs' world-wide profit levels were $2000m. In the United States one person in ten takes benzodiazepines for at least one week a year; and the consumption of these drugs has doubled in a decade. In 1974 U. S. doctors wrote twenty million prescriptions for one thousand million tablets of chlordiazepoxide (Librium) and sixty million prescriptions for three billion tablets of diazepam (Valium).[4]

'Valium for the prisoners of a society of stress', said the adverts which skillfully picked out the pressures on commuters, locked into wordless boredom and vacant faces, and housewives, imprisoned in towering blocks of flats, overpriced supermarkets, demanding children and an unsympathetic and exhausted spouse: 'Valium helps your patient enjoy his work. Formerly nervous and tense, he takes a greater interest in his job and is better able to meet and solve his daily problems.' If marriage is loveless, the streets without beauty and nights without peace, take a pill. Valium filled the space between the patient's desperation, the doctor's incompetence and the health service's disintegration. It provides the appearance of a solution satisfactory to all but in reality undermines the patients' ability to help themselves rather than strengthens it and debases the doctor's clinical skill. It confirms the mainly women patient's sense of themselves as failures, confirms an inner feeling that they are mad and, in the process, makes a very great deal more money for the shadowy millionaires of the drug multinationals.

The failure of reform

Drug companies are fond of painting pictures of the chaos that would ensue if any limitation on their freedom to operate like this is taken. However, even the very straightforward step of insisting that all N. H. S. prescriptions were made by the chemical title, which is insisted on during training but usually discarded under the pressure of practice, would alone save an estimated £50m. enough to build five brand new hospitals or 200 health centres. It is irresponsibility rather than clinical freedom to insist on prescribing, say, branded rather than formulary phenylbutazone, when the former costs four times as much as the latter. The further logical step is to make drug manufacture a public venture in the same way the N. H. S. is. The drug industry is effectively state-financed, since all the prescriptions signed by doctors are paid out of public taxation, so it ought to be in public ownership and concentrate on cheap, safe production of standardised drugs of proven value, and an increased and genuine research effort aimed to get to grips with the real problems. Although doctors would be livid initially – in the same way as they have reacted to every stage in the development of the N. H. S. – they, as before, would be the first to benefit from much simpler, medically sounder prescribing, instead of constantly attempting to evaluate new preparations on very sketchy and partial evidence. They would also benefit from the gigantic increase in resources available for staff and facilities.

However, many doctors seem to be wedded to the notion of freedom advocated by the drug companies. This notion is only an extreme example of the commercial capitalist values which surround and profit from the N. H. S. The companies are quite literally a law unto themselves and even quite determined efforts to impose some kind of responsibility on them has been unsuccessful. Since the Sainsbury Commission was set up in 1965, progress in controlling the industry has been very tiny and the Labour Party's 1976 proposals fail to restate some of the points made by Sainsbury, even though the intervening years has seen repeated conference, Labour Party and trade-union declarations. In fact, real action has been taken only twice and both times by a Tory government. At present, all price agreements are voluntary and the pharmaceutical industry is the only section of British industry not covered by the statutory Price Code and Price Commission. Indeed, drugs, as a proportion of spending, and the total number of prescriptions, are still growing rapidly, and yet government approaches are timid in the extreme. We are certainly prisoners, not of a society of stress, but one which profits from it.

7

Private practice

The appetite and the facilities of private practice fell somewhat after the introduction of the N. H. S. Even people who are very wealthy do not go out of their way to pay for something they can have for nothing. Nevertheless, the contract on which most hospital consultants were employed was usually tailored to allow part-time sessional attendance, to enable the doctors to see paying customers in non-N. H. S. time. A few doctors remained wholly in private practice but most had a few private patients who provided the financial jam on the N. H. S. bread and butter. In neither case is it really true that the patient got better medical care. A good doctor is a good doctor wherever he or she practises, and Harley Street has had perhaps more than its fair share of charlatans. But private practice *did* allow more time and personal consideration than is usually possible in N. H. S. conditions, including immediate appointments and surgery at convenient times.

When on the N. H. S. wards the consultant would rely heavily on his resident team and would be only too pleased to delegate to them, but in private practice this would simply divide up the proceeds. To put it at its most flattering, many doctors enjoyed the challenge of a more demanding middle-class private patient. Less charitably, they enjoyed being reminded that the skills they had acquired at public expense could still command a fee on the open market, and in a society which continues to accord moral value to price tags this will always be reassuring. There was relatively little private practice in fields with low financial prestige or in those which require ancillary facilities, themselves expensive. Apart from that hard core of doctors who have convinced themselves that a healthy doctor–patient relationship can only be really established if cash changes hands, many, while unwilling to take action against private practice, probably hoped that the N. H. S. would steadily improve to such a point that private practice would wither away. Few N. H. S. doctors I have met take much relish in exchanging their knowledge for money in a private transaction.

The rise of health insurance

Instead, two separate developments altered the terms on which private practice is carried out. First, a growing proportion of consultants, including the most scientifically eminent and those working in the professorial units in the teaching hospitals which had become the centres of the best hospital clinical medicine, worked full time. This, essential to a serious execution of clinical and academic duties nowadays, effectively redirected much of the enthusiasm which a previous generation put into developing their private clientele into raising N. H. S. standards. Where the full-time consultants were so eminent that private or overseas patients insisted on seeing them, fees, if charged, were paid into a department research or travelling fund rather than paid directly to the individual.

Second, some of the deficiencies in the N. H. S. detailed in previous chapters, enabled a renaissance of private medical insurance in the 1960s. The British United Provident Association (BUPA) became the largest of the organisations offering private medical care when some untoward illness developed. Although itself non-profitmaking, it is closely linked to supply companies who certainly are. Its schemes offered the best of both worlds: one was entitled to the full benefits of the N. H. S. but none of its disadvantages. If surgery was needed it could be taken in privacy, at an arranged time, executed by a surgeon of your choice. BUPA also provided access to preventative medicine of a commercial sort: screening and 'check-ups' designed for early detection of health hazards, which if detected are refered to the G. P.! Both these services ought to be available within the N. H. S. for everyone. In some well-endowed areas there is easy and flexible admission, more privacy for patients and the beginnings of universal screening schemes. But as, in general, waiting-lists becae longer and a harassed consultant was glimpsed rather than consulted, BUPA schemes, often arranged as part of managerial salary perks, became more attractive. For as doubts and horror stories about the N. H. S. became more vocal, it was security that the private schemes sold above all: 'Above all it means peace of mind that if you ever go into hospital you will have every comfort and care possible.' In this situation, part-time hospital consultants who in 1948 had wrung the right to admit their private patients to beds in the hospital to which they had been appointed were in a commanding position. Bevan had choked the profession's mouth with pay-beds as well as gold, and the former had turned out to be more valuable.

In the last ten years the pattern has been established of part-time consultants negotiating directly with private insurance schemes, which in turn can offer companies block insurance schemes complete with tax relief. BUPA doubled its membership by this means in the first half of the 1970s and the total of patients now covered by private insurance is 4 per cent of the population and at the present rate of growth will have increased to between 10–15 per cent in ten years. The number of part-time consultants has increased from 2463 in 1949 to 4297 in 1970. Hugh Ewell, marketing director of BUPA, states: 'As I see it, the individual subscriber to a provident scheme is going to be increasingly rare. And those who do will be essentially the bad risks. Instead there will be increasing moves towards company and occupational schemes, a move which started a few years ago and is now escalating.'[1] Manual workers are left with the 'cash-in-hospital' providential schemes with their lurid one-page advertisements and copious fine print.

About 30 per cent of total benefit payments accrue to the medical attendant; of this 90 per cent goes to the surgeons and anaesthetists. There remain close links between the medical establishment and the private section, as evidenced by the gusto with which the B. M. A. identified with 'The Campaign for Independence in Medicine', a well-financed body which plastered Britain's medical walls with posters attempting to prove the removal of pay-beds from N. H. S. hospitals was the beginning of an era of state tyranny and the suppression of the medical profession.

The N. H. S. pay-beds

The 1946 Act bound the Minister to provide, to such an extent as he considered necessary to meet all reasonable requirements, hospital accommodation for private work. The Health Service and Public Health Act of 1968 re-asserted that, at the Minister's discretion, this should continue. By 1970 about 122,000 patients were seen annually in just under 5000 beds inside the N. H. S., with the thirteen London teaching hospitals providing 15 per cent of the total beds. The proportion of pay-beds has kept fairly constant at one in a hundred of total beds, but such is the nature of the instant service they offer that they lie empty for over half the year. The private beds in the N. H. S. were only a quarter of the number existing outside in independent nursing homes and private hospitals. But their particular relationship to N. H. S. facilities enabled them to tap resources in a number of quite subtle but important ways, which all stem from the part-time consultants' dual role, with its ability to both practise privately and maintain their positions in the N. H. S.

The most obvious abuse resulting from the double position does not even require a pay-bed. It is the habit of seeing a private patient on a fee-paid consultation and then expediting that patient's N. H. S. admission for routine surgery. The use of N. H. S. facilities and personnel for private surgery is most resented by hospital staff. My first direct experience of this was overhearing one houseman delightedly tell his successor that there was a chance once a month to go and hold the chief's retractor in the London Clinic; such was the man's sense of loyalty and careerism he considered this unpaid duty a positive privilege. But the House of Commons Committee that investigated private practice in the N. H. S. heard evidence from a junior doctor about the eye department, where 'The consultant operated on the private patients in the Ophthalmic Department operating theatre after the afternoon's NHS list had been finished. The regular nursing staff were in attendance at the private operations for which extra duty they received an occasional box of confectionery.' The consultant probably got £400 for his work. The nurses got sweets, but the people who cleaned the theatre, washed and packed the linen and cleared up the mess got nothing. A senior laboratory technician reported that 'The arrival of a single "private" specimen, which must invariably be done "straight away", throws the whole routine into chaos.' When it was questioned, he received the reply that private-practice work was 'pure profit' and should not therefore be interrupted. Until recently the rate charged for private N. H. S. was below cost and certainly made no allowance for capital costs – probably £20,000 per bed. Even then a surprising proportion of N. H. S. pay-bed patients defaulted on their bills! In North-west Thames, for example, over £43,811 was owing in bad debts in 1975–6.

N. H. S. equipment, such as sterile instrument packs and specialised technical devices (private theatres are often very badly equipped) are borrowed commonly and I have several times seen anaesthetists vanishing with a handful of syringes, drugs and, occasionally, anaesthetic fluids. Now, most employees of big institutions 'borrow' odd bits and pieces and think it part of the perks. But it seems somewhat unfair that a hungry nurse can be reprimanded for finishing up a patient's meal and a domestic fired for taking home a sliced loaf which would otherwise go mouldy, but when consultants help themselves to N. H. S. facilities they are somehow defending clinical freedom. To operate a double standard is always unpleasant but it becomes especially so when it is clear the comfort of one level is being achieved at the expense of lower standards and longer waits for the other, and that financial ambition is being larded with a great deal of lofty humbug uttered by people the *Lancet* called 'The resolute defenders of self-interest.' The private patients in the N. H. S. were getting a bargain, the consultants were keeping quiet and doing very nicely out of it, and in the process the chances of an N. H. S. patient were worsening remorselessly. In reality the best way to abolish private practice altogether would be to improve the N. H. S. so that the Hackney General was raised to the level of Addenbrookes or Edinburgh Royal. Of course private medicine flourishes because precisely the reverse is happening and most people realise it, even if the government refuses to admit it.

Direct action

However, the pay-beds issue seemed likely to quietly simmer on without anything very much being done, a token to be volleyed back and forth across the ideological fence. The 1974 Labour Party manifesto included a promise to phase out pay-beds, and a prolonged and inconclusive committee under David Owen's chairmanship was to discuss the matter. Meanwhile, hospital workers, in the course of their first disastrously defeated national strike in 1972, had discovered that refusing the extra chores for the private patients produced an unprecedented response from management. Whereas most union action had inevitably inconvenienced the ill public and only put pressure on the employers (the government) in a very indirect fashion, the ban on private patients hit the pockets of the most influential consultants, who made their feelings felt in no uncertain terms to local and national management.

This original tactic lasted after the strike was defeated, more as a way to exert selective industrial pressure than any campaign against private practice itself. At the Brook Hospital in South London it was carried on after the strike, which, despite a poor settlement, had greatly enhanced the organisation and morale of the ancillary workers. The branch secretaries said:

It started from the strike in March. We thought it was a good idea to have one or two irons in the fire which we could continue with after the strike. Several people during the strike had said they thought that private patients should not be using the facilities of NHS hospitals. If we haven't got an effective health service, it's because the government haven't made it an effective health service. In banning Private Practice, as we see it, we are fighting for everyone in the country – even those who have the money to afford private schemes. To get treatment quickly people need to pay again, which they shouldn't have to. At the other end of the scale the patient who is already paying the stamp is denied this treatment because he can't afford it – but he's already paid for it. What they're doing is defining the health service in two ways. You're getting a mediocre service for the poor people and a super-effective service for the rich people.[2]

The entire Wessex region began operating a ban, based on Portsmouth, from March 1973. Although there were only thirty beds in the city, these cater for over 2000 individuals during one year – over half the city's waiting-list. There, and at the Hammersmith Hospital soon after, it proved a considerable success. Attempts to smuggle in anonymous private patients were blocked by the joint vigilance of porters, domestics, nurses, sympathetic doctors, N. H. S. patients and their visitors, switchboard operators and pathology laboratory technicians. Private patients who could not resist bragging about their status instead found themselves rumbled. The kitchen staff refused to concoct the special meals for the private patients. At Hammersmith, where private patients were put on general wards, the union stewards issued a regularly updated list of private patients, including their pseudonyms, so that all departments involved in the action could accurately refuse service, transport or investigation. Most workers were only too pleased to unload the extra chores involved in working for private patients. The hospital management, who had previously scoffed at the union claims that extra attention for private patients was preventing service to the rest, found out for itself quite what was involved. Most important, the private beds were cleared for N. H. S. patients.

But these initiatives remained local and unofficial despite attempts to spread the word until a crisis suddenly blew up on the fifteenth floor of the new Charing Cross Hospital in July 1976, a crisis which suddenly plummetted the pay-bed anomaly back into the national headlines. Once again NUPE members had begun to put pressure on the private section, particularly in view of the slowness in introducing the 'consolidated' waiting-lists which had been promised since 1 January to guarantee that queue-jumping unrelated to medical urgency was curtailed. At Charing Cross, the consultants, already in dispute with Barbara Castle (then the Minister of Health, whose sex, let alone her politics, they seemed to resent) over the renewal of their contracts, were organised and ready to make an issue of it.

The doctors reply

Before even the threat was issued to take direct action to encourage the phasing-out process along the lines of the manifesto of the government as well as the long-standing policies of the Labour Party, the T. U. C. and most of the hospital unions, the consultants had liaised with the B. M. A. Council – who had informally warned Castle. When the ancillary workers announced they would cease to supply meals to private patients, the consultants counter-blasted that they would continue private practice by any means necessary and their patients would not be moved. A large B. M. A. delegation assembled hastily for a ten-hour negotiating session to announce to Mrs Castle that if concessions were made then nation-wide 'sanctions' would be taken and they would withdraw from the Owen working party. It transpired that a combat section of the B. M. A. had in fact been preparing documentation on the sanctions for some months. Sanctions had been first mentioned in the 1965 dispute over the conditions of general practice and brandished again in the 1970 confrontation with the review body. In both cases it had been necessary for the B. M. A. to transmogrify into a phantom association called the British Medical Guild in order to act like a union. The sanctions always started with 'non-co-operation', which usually meant refusing things that the doctors did not like very much doing in the first place, always backed with the threat of withdrawing from the N. H. S. In 1970 the B. M. A. had stockpiled undated resignations to this effect.

The effectiveness of the sanctions in this instance is rather hard to evaluate. They were only half-heartedly executed by the full-timers who did most of the work and many 'nine to eleven' consultants, the force behind the B. M. A., had never devoted that proportion of their time to N. H. S. work anyway. Many hospitals were so accustomed to getting along without the physical presence of part-time consultants that sanctions made relatively little difference, except to pile up the waiting-list still further and silt up the beds. Many juniors resented being assumed to support their consultants on this issue, when in some cases consultants had failed to suport their protest against juniors' hours and pay.

The issue had very little immediate impact on G. P.s, who had long since lost any direct access to hospital beds, pay or otherwise. The B. M. A. has always tended to respond to any government regulation of private medicine with certain high-sounding stock phrases: 'putting party ideology before the community's interest' (anything done by a Labour Minister); the ever-present 'threat to clinical freedom' (doctors' right to do what they like with other people's money); and 'a malicious attempt at social levelling'. Dr H. Fidler, Chairman of the Private Practice Committee, told the Hull Conference that 'If we lose this freedom . . . the medical profession is finished. Even worse, this country is finished.' The *Daily Telegraph* pontificated on 'the exhibitionist rantings of the tedious Mrs Esther Brookstone', the *Daily Mail* on 'the battling grannie' – ironically, as the Secretary of NUPE at Charing Cross was well known as a staunch supporter of the conservative wing of her union. Her elevation to political stardom was the result of the Charing Cross consultants' militancy, not her own, which was exercised mainly in restraining those for whom, in her words, 'strikes had become an action for their own sake, not to achieve anything, but to be "militant", and many of us have been sickened by those who have become known as the "death and glory" boys – our death and their glory!'[3]

Even the B. M. A. were a little embarrassed over the issue; 'The most difficult case to present convincingly to the public. At first glance it smacks too much of the defence of privilege.' A columnist in a G. P.s' newspaper voiced some of the reservations on the invisible subsidy given to the pay-beds, suggesting they should be charged 'at their true cost, with the capital element fully reflected'. 'If the middle classes,' he added, 'are to be protected from the knowledge of the astronomical costs of providing full health care, how can the public at large ever understand the costs involved?.'A speaker at the B. M. A. Annual Meeting expressed his misgivings: '[He] would be branded as a heretic but [he] was not convinced of the need for private beds in the NHS hospitals. [He] was not prepared to take militant action on this matter and neither were [his] general practitioner colleagues.' The head of one of the larger private hospital groups – American Medical International – was even more blunt: 'Private beds should have been phased out of the NHS long ago. They are an anomaly.'

Meanwhile, despite Barbara Castle's direct appeal to hospital ancillary workers to return to work ('While I can understand the feelings of the staff, I cannot condone the action they are taking'), the union action spread very rapidly through the informal rank-and-file networks. The action was taken up in July 1974 at St George's at Hyde Park, St George's in Tooting, the Atkinson Morely in Wimbledon, and the Royal Dental in Leicester Square, as well as over a hundred Northern hospitals, centred on the West Yorkshire hospitals grouped around Leeds, Pontefract and Huddersfield, some of which had been operating an informal ban for several months. In most cases the number of patients affected was very low. It was more a public declaration of intent, with the prospect of local talks which might withdraw cooking and laundry facilities (which the management usually quickly supplied).

Nevertheless, it required the usually male, usually portering and technical NUPE stewards to canvass support of the mainly women laundry and catering staff, and to explain the issue to ward nurses and the other N. H. S. patients, who, in hospitals where private patients shared open parts with them, were often affected too. In some cases leaflets were dished out to patients instead of menus.

The unionists were well aware of the importance of the private-patient issue. An unofficial union guide summarises their case clearly:

> Private practice in the NHS benefits a minority of patients (4 per cent), a minority of doctors (7,000 out of 60,000) and virtually no nurses, technicians or ancillaries. Private patients are subsidised by unrealistically low charges for the use of NHS facilities. They are able to jump the long waiting lists because they have money. Private practice is about greed more than need, it would be unnecessary if the NHS were improved instead of cut. Private patients are socially irresponsible and make it in the doctors' interests to over-investigate, over-treat and do unnecessary surgery. It would never pay private practice to preach preventative medicine.

Private practice: the implications

The consultants were right to sense a more general resentment surfacing in the hospitals. It was a conflict between low-paid, undervalued but essential hospital workers, and those consultants who still acted as a law unto themselves and gave the impression that the hospital was lucky to have their services at all. It was this survival of the 'honorary' attitudes, that automatic sense of power a doctor attained simply from offering his services, the older traditions of subservience, deference and obligation, of medicine as a single-handed elite craft skill, which were all embodied in the persistence of private practice. There was, too, the suspicion that the neglect of the N. H. S. was, in some obscure sense, interrelated to the rise of private practice. In the conflict all those little slights and abruptnesses to which some consultants feel themselves entitled, the tantrums in theatre and the explosions over missing X-rays were remembered.

Far from the inaccurate malice which the *Daily Telegraph* suspected was being aimed by planted Marxists, the willingness of ordinary members to take direct industrial action against pay-beds (which far outstripped the expectations of even the politically minded stewards) reflected a real concern about fairness in medicine, and was a protest against the pyramid of power inside hospitals which most people resent but few have the valour to defy. Witness the *British Medical Journal*:

> Since the NHS was established 'its professional groups, especially doctors, have accepted their dual role as 'worker-directors' as a matter of course. . . .' They have used [it continued, poker-faced], this power responsibly and certainly in an apolitical fashion. But as dons and teachers have already discovered, that traditional authority is being challenged – and from a political platform.

Direct action of this kind, whose implications go further than the money-militancy of traditional trade-union action, expresses a political questioning that goes beyond the cross on the ballot paper every general election. As the hospital workers pointed out gleefully, the pay-bed business had been through all the democratic motions, was duly offered in the Labour Party's manifesto on which they had won the election, and *still* nothing happened. As *The Times* put it, 'Labour Party policy is that private beds should be phased out, but as recently as last February, all appearances were that there was no great urgency about starting. All that was changed, by the bans on private patients by non-medical staff.'

The protest was also aimed at the Labour Party and the union officials. It was not just against their inactivity and lack of resolution about their own resolutions, repeated annually as evidence of their righteousness rather than as any possible guide to action, but, in a curious way, Barbara Castle's sudden concern about private beds too, for, in truth, it was an ideal issue on which to seem radical in the Bevan idiom, to give the appearance of challenging the medical establishment without spending a farthing. In perspective, it enabled the Labour Party to enter its first phase of the cutbacks in the N. H. S. unnoticed, indeed radiant in the reflected glow of the beds.

Ultimately, the pay-beds *are* a side issue, albeit an important one, in the over-all crisis in the National Health Service. It enabled union presidents to make radical-sounding orations at the seaside instead of really tackling the issue of raising basic wage rates. It gave the Labour Party a veneer of egalitarianism on health while they continued to crow about the N. H. S.'s vanishing virtues while depriving it of the resources which might make them possible. It gave the B. M. A. the chance to bang the drum of clinical freedom. It *was* true that many poor and middle-class people had saved for health insurance not out of any sense of elitism but because of first-hand experience of its own decline in quality and low respect for patient convenience, which the Labour Party, in power for fourteen out of the first thirty years of the N. H. S.'s existence, has allowed.

The solution?

In the eventual compromise negotiated by Lord Goodman, private practice emerged considerably strengthened. Rather than stating a case on principle against private medicine, the compromise suggests it is perfectly acceptable as long as it takes place outside N. H. S. premises, an out-of-sight, out-of-mind attitude which has given the go ahead for the biggest burst of speculative commercial hospital building since the Victorian age. The Independent Hospital Group was founded in November 1974, under the wing of BUPA, to co-ordinate the provision of private facilities outside the N. H. S. As Jack Massey, Chairman of Kentucky Fried Chicken, who resigned to become head of the Hospital Corporation of America, noted, 'The growth potential in hospitals is unlimited: its even better than Kentucky Fried Chicken.'[4]

The Times reported Dr Stanley Balfour-Lynn of American Health International, which runs the Harley Street Clinic, as saying that 'Up to 20 private hospitals costing a total of £60 million could be built in Britain within two to three years.' He said the money would come from British institutions and from the pension funds of big unions. He declined to name names, but said that the money was available if needed. Private medicine would show a 'very good return'. Between ten and twenty private hospitals could be built in two to three years at a cost of £3 million or so each. They would be built 'if the need was there and we had reassurances that Barbara Castle is not going to do anything stupid about private medicine. We would want some certainty that she wouldn't go further than she says.' The older picture of private facilities often operating on a non-commercial basis by established charities or religious orders is being changed into one where hospital-building is frankly profit-orientated and aimed openly at attracting patients from overseas. The Wellington Hospital, which cost £54 million and has ninety-eight beds, was opened in July 1974. There is a staffing ratio of one and a half nurses per patient as well as electronically controlled beds, air conditioning, a telephone and a wine list (including Chateau Mouton Rothschild at £25.60 a bottle). Nurses are paid at 10 per cent above Whitley rates with good subsidised housing, free luxury food and no overtime. Ancillary staff wages were correspondingly higher: £60 for a porter with experience in driving Rolls-Royces, and £72 for a waiter familiar with silver service. The Harley Street Clinic is a £1.65 million construction in Harley and Wimpole Streets, three-quarters owned by an American firm, American Medical International Inc., which specialises in acquiring and reconstructing clinics in Europe. In November 1974 BUPA opened their first private hospital – the Florence Nightingale in Marylebone. The medical tycoon, the property speculator and profit-hungry investment company are an unsavoury alliance, their ethical approach well conveyed in an advertisement in the *Financial Times*: 'think it over, Mr Chairman. . . . Why not own a private hospital close to Harley Street. . . . The annual gross income on beds alone is almost £2,500,000 plus all the extras – and no advertising costs! Ask any consultant!'

It was commerce and concessions which finished off what the hospital workers' honest indignation started. Lord Goodman, who was appointed by Harold Wilson to act as a go-between with the B. M. A., wrote to *The Times* on 27 April 1976, boasting about the extent the Castle Bill had been watered down:

the Bill is hardly recognisable as the offspring of the Consultative Document of August 1975. It reflects massive concessions, may I say achieved by the tenacity of the leaders of the profession principally in the establishment of an Independent Health Service Board. . . . It is I think common knowledge that the figure of 1,000 beds was determined as one based on a very large measure of agreement that they were redundant and many of them already in NHS use. . . . If this Bill is approved by Parliament I believe it provides a secure base for private medicine and a springboard for its continuation and I hope enlargement.

Once the pressure of direct action on the wards was removed, and the issue itself removed to the rarified air of 'committeedom', its meaning was reversed. An instinctive move towards fairness ended up in strengthening privilege. Barbara Castle ended up stating that her measures were 'an expression of the Government's commitment to the maintenance of private practice in this country'.[5]

8
Health trade unionism

Over the past five years in Britain, hospital trade unions have emerged from their shadowy existence somewhere in the wings of the N. H. S. to the centre of the political stage. From a situation in which industrial action was virtually unknown, even on wage issues, by 1977 every grade of hospital staff had taken some sort of national strike action, including direct action for and against the retention of private pay-beds within N. H. S. hospital wards, strike protest against government welfare policy, pickets of hospital workers against proposed stiffening of the abortion laws, a multitude of disputes over hours, conditions and discipline, and finally action against 'the cuts' in defence of the service itself. This has been part of the general post-war growth of trade unionism among the predominantly female employees of the Welfare State, whose effective boss is the Treasury, and whose work, in the schools, hospitals, nurseries and welfare centres, has been, almost because it was concerned with caring rather than producing for profit, very lowly paid. Like a surf-board rider the expansion of welfare jobs hurtled forward even as the economic wave that carried it crumpled within. The N. H. S. continued to gobble up labour long after the size of the industrial work-force was restricted forcibly, giving hospital trade unionism a new weight and political importance within the labour movement.

This growth was not an orderly, automatic and respectable expansion but had been punctuated with strikes, marches and battles, with management savouring much more of the militancy of the mines and work-shops than the obedient, even pleading, tones built in to the Whitley Council system. Now the boom economy which had created the new welfare industries was in reverse gear, the unions that grew with them will face their most severe test and their platform rhetoric will go under challenge. Paradoxically these unions, in their existing structures, are unusually undemocratic, male-dominated and hostile to any militancy which might escape their head offices' control or damage the electoral prospects of the Labour Party.

'Whitleyism'

The establishment of the N. H. S. brought automatic recognition of the right of all hospital workers to join a union of their choice. The unions, very roughly represented according to membership, meet nationally to negotiate over conditions of service in bodies known as Whitley Councils, ten separate but linked bodies covering the different grades of hospital worker. This method of wage bargaining applies generally in the public sector in Britain and was consciously introduced as a check to the vigorous local bargaining which was the backbone of the syndicalist movement earlier in the century. Whitley himself was a Halifax cotton-spinner and although the terms of the Commission he headed in 1916 were mildly intended to 'make and consider suggestions for securing a permanent improvement in the relations between employers and workmen', they reflected an urgent need for securing industrial peace by some compulsory system of negotiation which would regain the initiative from the shop-floor. Not only had strike levels risen to record heights in the years immediately before 1914, but workers, animated by the syndicalist idea of workers' control, regarding nationalisation as the employers' last ditch and suspicious of their own leaders' respectability, were looking more to the revolutionary advocates of soviets than the top-hatted leaders of craft unionism. J. T. Murphy, one of the most forceful advocates of the soviet conception, saw the aim of Whitley's Committee clearly as 'to kill the workshop movement as an independent movement'.

But while Whitley cut little ice with industrial workers, it was a godsend to weaker unions like NUPE and NALGO who clung on to the coat tail of its legal recognition of a joint bargaining structure to spread trade unionism peacefully.

While Whitleyism guarantees the right to union membership, it is stamped with a very restricted notion of union activity. Rights granted rather than won often remain nominal. Although the Whitley Council handbook rules cover hospital workers' conditions in extraordinary complexity it remains an abstraction. Often hospital workers would have to undertake great battles to extract rights which were supposed to exist anyway. Until quite recently union life centred on an area-wide branch meeting infrequently in the evening. Sometimes the officials were retired and in some cases in receipt of a personal bounty according to the size of the membership – which positively encouraged them to maintain large and unwieldy branches. The rank-and-file members' subscriptions to the union was just another deduction from the wage packet, a possible source of cheap insurance or travel, or a useful counter-threat in disciplinary cases. Once a year 'their' leader would be on television, either making dire threats of disruption or more often exaggerated claims for recently negotiated settlements.

NUPE

The consequences of Whitleyism, trade unionism from above, are clearly seen in the National Union of Public Employees (NUPE), the biggest hospital union, which organises manual workers in four main sections: local authorities, hospitals, universities and water authorities. It has about 250,000 hospital members (including porters, domestic workers, ward-cleaners, chefs, cooks, kitchen workers, telephonists, gardeners, laundry workers, and workers in many other manual trades, as well as a growing number of nurses) and grew out of a union for all London municipal employees founded by a London socialist sewage worker in 1888. By and large its hospital members simply tagged behind the settlements negotiated with the local-authority manual workers. Although the union grew enormously with the foundation of the N. H. S., the only major industrial action it took was in 1956 when mass meetings of women domestics in London forced the union to take up the struggle for the 44-hour work week which had been granted to every other industry and service in 1953. In most hospitals, union dues were checked off automatically by management, union meetings were infrequent, and the officers of the local branch tended to be re-elected without change or challenge, often simply because of the status of their hospital job rather than their commitment to unionism. The unelected full-time officers of the union seemed to see their role as almost philanthropic, looking after 'their' hospital workers. Its national leaders have traditionally been drawn from outside the union: Jack Wills, a building worker, Bryn Roberts, a miner, and Sydney Hill, an engineer. Its present (1978) general secretary was appointed to the union staff at the age of 16 and, apart from war service, has worked for the union all his life. Each general secretary appears to have personally groomed his successor in an almost Roman fashion.

The union's national membership was 105,000 members at the end of the Second World War. By 1955 it had 200,000 and was the ninth largest in the T. U. C. By 1975 there were 508,000 and over the next eighteen months alone the membership was increased by 22 per cent to a total of 620,806. As a proportion of the membership women rose even more rapidly, from one-half in 1968 to two-thirds in 1975, almost three-quarters of the 301,000 members signed up. Yet only two of its 122 appointed officials and six of its twenty-six executive members are women. As a woman member put the paradox rather delicately: 'The union is strong on positive discrimination for women, even if it appears in strange ways sometimes – the branch with the best level of women's activity, i.e. recruitment of women, receives the silver rose bowl!' Certainly until the union's first national strike in 1972–3, most members had only the most passive connection and vague understanding of their own union, which was run for them by professionals. The results were exceptionally low basic wages for a fairly demoralised membership who were forced to work enormous lengths of overtime to earn a living wage. Equal pay existed: it was equally low for men and women.

COHSE

The Confederation of Health Service Employees (COHSE) is in theory the industrial union for the N. H. S., but in practice its real base is among the predominantly male mental-hospital nurses and some of the more senior nurses in the general hospitals. A militant campaigner among the nurses after the establishment of the N. H. S., COHSE was recently disaffiliated from the T. U. C. during the battle against the Conservative government's Industrial Relations Act for registering itself on the official government roll which the majority of trade unions were boycotting. In terms of its local weakness, COHSE suffered from all the defects of NUPE in more acute form. None the less, the conditions of its members were so terrible that there were still occasional muffled COHSE explosions, like that led by mental nurses from Senegal and Mauritius at the Leavensden Hospital, the largest mental hospital in Britain, in 1970. Among their complaints then were hostels infested with mice, lack of heating or any cooking facilities, even a shortage of chairs in rest-rooms. Even here the branch secretaries' reaction when the nurses themselves handed in their resignations was merely that 'The union has done everything it can to stop a mass walk-out . . . although the nurses do not have our official backing they have our sympathy.'

Other unions

The Transport and General Workers' Union, the leftish general workers' union, organises some hospitals, notably in Scotland and the North, but this seems to be a matter of chance. The General and Municipal Workers' Union, a notoriously undemocratic and right-wing general union, also has a base in some hospitals. Curiously, these plus NUPE and COHSE, with widely differing memberships, have equal votes on the Whitley Council covering ancillary workers. It consists of sixteen trade-union representatives and nineteen management representatives, of whom sixteen are from various N. H. S. governing bodies and three appointed by the D. H. S. S. The management and the D. H. S. S. have a permanent majority but this is scarcely needed since all decisions on money matters rest with the Treasury official in attendance and all decisions are arrived at by consensus anyway. Even more curiously, in 1978 Alan Fisher sat on the staff side of the Ancillary Whitley Council but on the management side of the London White Collar Electricity Workers Whitley Council and was a director of British Airways into the bargain.

Nurses

Nurses were undoubtedly the most exploited section of N. H. S. workers, especially student nurses, who in 1970 amounted to over half of nurses working on the wards. A first-year student nurse's take-home 'training allowance' was then between £6 and £7. This was for an official 42-hour week which was invariably extended, because no handover time was allowed or because it was customary to do extra time if ward work was not finished, and often included a shift split into two – which manages to ruin the whole day. It also automatically involved night and week-end work with no extra payment. According to a 1969 amendment of the *Nurses' Rules*, the maximum amount of sick or compassionate leave allowed a student nurse amounted to one week a year. Student nurses would often listen to lectures, even sit examinations, after a full night on duty. Life takes place within the nursing home: a survey of 800 Malaysian student nurses in London found television the main entertainment for 86 per cent of nurses.

Much ward work was still swamped in unexplained routine. Indeed there would often be one routine for the tutor sister and quite another to please the sister on the ward. The combined effect of a heavy and difficult work-load, petty discipline and lack of qualified staff makes the job very wearing. A student nurse wrote in despair:

A student nurse with only a single month's training finds herself alone at night with pretty well full responsibility for a whole ward of patients. She is frightened – but not just of making mistakes. She is frightened of calling her superior, engaged elsewhere, even in an emergency. So the student does make some mistakes. The next day she is severely reprimanded – as if a young girl learning about nursing doesn't punish herself enough for not doing all she might have done for her patients. The next night she is back on the same ward, in the same situation, with the same fears. She makes further mistakes. She goes away. No one knows what has happened to her or where she has gone. She's just another statistic in the GNC wastage rates.

Until quite recently the nurses have only rarely joined the industrial unions, preferring instead membership in professional bodies like the Royal College of Nursing (R.C.N.) and the Royal College of Midwives which combine educational and professional functions with some dabbling in wage negotiation. These bodies are dominated by senior nurses and there is no effective and democratic control by student and ward nurses. Thus, when the rank-and-file pressure inside the R.C.N. at the 1969 conference led to the setting up of the 'Raise the Roof' campaign for higher pay, a 38-hour week and proper student status for trainee nurses, the campaign was carried out along strictly controlled and respectable lines by the senior R.C.N. members who themselves had imposed some of the petty restrictions. One nurse wrote:

The whole campaign was controlled from the top. The slogans and demands were already prepared. The meetings were dominated by speakers from the platform – the establishment – and any inde-pendent militant spirit was crushed wherever possible. The nurses were told they could not strike; we were not left to think about this and decide for ourselves – even though many possibly would not anyway. Eventually most nurses stopped attending the meetings – they could not be bothered to be talked at yet again.

The negotiations resulted in an equally top-heavy settlement. Although the average pay rise awarded in April 1971 was 20 per cent, the upper echelons did relatively better, with salaries jumping from £2500 to £3700, than the staff nurses, who only moved from £18 to £23 a week, and the student nurses with a rise of £1.50. This rise was almost immediately absorbed by increases in lodging and food charges and the taxman's whack.

Clerical workers

Hospital clerical workers and administrators also join a mixture of professional and trade-union bodies, but the National Association of the Local Government Officers (NALGO), the militant Town Hall union, has increasingly become dominant. NALGO's origins were conservative. It was founded in 1905 as a frankly Tory association of Town Hall clerks. Its ounder, Herbert Bain, later became national agent for the Conservative Party, and its first paid national secretary stated that 'anything savouring of trade unionism is nausea to the Local Government Officer and his Association'. It only really began to grow after the House of Lords found in favour of the Whitley system in Town Halls as late as 1942, which enabled the establishment of suitable national salary scales for local-government officers. A rank-and-file revolt began against the 1969 local government settlement and this affected the N. H. S. membership, and became embodied in the successful rank-and-file body, the Nalgo Action Group'. In 1977 the union had 357,942 male members and 267,221 female. Nevertheless, only seventeen out of 191 officials, five out of sixty-six executive members and five out of seventy-four T.U.C. delegates were women.

A scattering of industrial and craft unions cover the skilled manual tradesmen such as electricians, plumbers, builders, and the silver and gold trades workers inside hospitals. These craft unions, which have been increasingly attempting to negotiate wages directly with the D. H. S. S., have often provided a core of trade-union experience within hospitals.

Doctors

Doctors have traditionally had a different negotiating procedure, the Review Body system. At periodical intervals, when professional discontent reaches a certain point, an independent group of members of the establishment, usually chaired by a retired managing director, takes evidence from all interested bodies and submits an award to the Prime Minister of the day who can accept, modify, postpone or reject it. The Review Body system resulted from the Pilkington Commission in 1960. It was to be that most elusive of beasts, the 'independent' body whose recommendations could be rejected by the government of the day 'only very reluctantly and for the most compelling reasons'. Nevertheless, the seventh Kindersley Review Body report and recommendations were deferred and then not paid in full and in 1970 the whole Review Body resigned when its recommendations were halved. It has served as an indirect instrument of government incomes policy and produced not only the lowest-paid doctors in Western Europe but also a steady fall of doctors' incomes relative to other British professions.

Despite regular exasperated uprisings and splits, the effectively dominant representative body remains the British Medical Association, not unfairly called the 'Tory Party at the bedside'. The Junior Hospital Doctors Association emerged in the mid-1960s to dramatise the conditions of house officers undertaking their compulsory pre-registration jobs. They drew public attention to this almost medieval apprenticeship and the long hours, poor residential conditions, and bad educational facilities for registrars, who were still undergoing hospital-based postgraduate specialist education but were more often used as cheap medical labour. More recently the provincial consultants (the heads of the hospital clinical teams) have broken away from what they see as an unrepresentative and London teaching-hospital-biased B. M. A. elite. The Medical Practitioners Union, the only genuine trade union operating among doctors, has traditionally been based on the general practitioners, but has recently expanded briskly among more radically minded hospital juniors as part of the general spread of trade unionism among white-collar workers in Britain. The Medical Practitioners Union (M. P. U.) is now a subsection of the Association of Scientific Technical and Management Staffs, the fastest growing of the white-collar unions which organise in insurance, research and technical laboratories, but whose membership includes airline pilots, executives, and office workers as well, and totals over 400,000. Its base in the hospitals is among medical technicians, pharmacists, biochemists, physiological-measurement technicians and junior doctors. It has traditionally campaigned for reform of Whitleyism, more spending on the N. H. S.

and a proper occupational health service in view of the particularly high health risks in hospitals.

The M. P. U. was formed in 1914 from an organisation of doctors supporting a state medical service. Its members were mainly drawn from 'panel' doctors who considered the B. M. A. did not represent their interests. After the First World War it affiliated to the T. U. C. and remained predominantly a G. P. organisation until it joined A. S. T. M. S. in 1971. Until the 1970s the B. M. A., while claiming exclusive rights to negotiate for doctors, was violently hostile to trade unions, especially, heaven forbid, unions for doctors.

Before 1970, despite a fair degree of muttering and grumbling, none of these unions seriously attempted to use industrial action to improve wages or conditions. The emphasis was still on the quality of the negotiators rather than the potential power of the membership. In this respect there was not such a great difference between those unions which adopted left-wing resolutions at their annual conferences and those which passed right-wing pronouncements. The lack of effective hospital organisation has fostered a measure of importance for the national leadership which in some cases borders on megalomania. In the near-petulant self-esteem and suiting of Clive Jenkins, the comic timing of Alan Fisher with his trace of the Lancastrian lady-killer, or for that manner the guttural Russian-Brooklyn oratory of Leon Davis, the head of Local 1166 of the New York hospital workers union, their personality or rather their skill at performance somehow *becomes* the union. Therefore, although themselves left-wing in sympathies, all three react with near-hysteria to internal radical criticism, since such is the degree of over-personalisation and absence of real democracy an attack on them *is* an attack on the union. Trade unions became a servant of their machines: hence the full-timer, the headed notepaper, the annual conference, and the unreadable magazine with its picture of presentations for long-serving officers lying around in unsold bundles. Women workers, migrant workers and most male workers who lack previous trade-union experience were to this extent outsiders in their own union, whose wage bargaining was conducted in almost incomprehensible complexity by professional management, professional union full-timers and civil servants, who had more in common with each other than with hospital workers.

When hospital managers and union full-timers meet, it is obvious how similar they are, in sex, in clothes, in that particular managerial habit or skill of making things sound more complicated than they really are. On the other hand, what is remarkable about the health workers the union leaders represent is their diversity. Everything that links the professionals is different: colour, size, shape, nationality, personality and temperament. Scuffed suits and patterned ties trying to deal with a sea of differences; wiry gay telephonists, gigantic cooks from Barbados, disabled X-ray porters, sardonic Catholic staff nurses, effusive impatient Spanish ward maids, graceful giggling Thai ward nurses, Home Counties house doctors busily flapping their white coats, and pathology technicians in grubbier coats figuring out their overtime and quick routes to the local.

A hospital has a single aim which is carried out in a multitude of different but interdependent labour processes, each with its own species of grievance: the student nurse wants another gas-ring in the sitting-room, the night porters are worried about their overtime, the assistant orthopaedic appliance maker wants upgrading. It has only been as the rank-and-file hospital unions have taken up day-to-day issues that they have dented the rigid classifications of skills and jobs that keep all health workers compartmentalised, and the union has taken on a real meaning in the hospital. And to do this they have had to fashion their own informal union structures.

Ancillary workers' strikes 1970–3

The first sign of a different mood came from the underpaid and under-appreciated ancillary workers. In 1970 an unofficial strike broke out in the Royal Free Hospital in London, an establishment founded by women suffragette doctors. The Cinderellas of the hospital service, the porters, theatre technicians, domestics, telephonists and boilermen, went on a one-day strike, joined by union members in St Mary's and Bethnal Green Hospitals. The mixture of caution and desperate impatience can be seen in one of the leaflets distributed at the Royal Free Hospital:

> We apologise for any inconvenience this may cause you, but as you know our basic wage in the hospital service is scandalous considering today's cost of living, and our conditions of service leave much to be desired, like the fact that we have to work seven years before we get three weeks' annual holiday.

The basic rates for married hospital workers were still £14, £2.50 under the national minimum wage suggested by the T.U.C.

By the autumn of 1972, many hospital ancillary workers were actually getting basic wages below the official government 'poverty line' and would have done better financially if they had ceased working and drew unemployment and social-security benefits. Then all the major hospitals in Bristol were stopped by a walk-out, a quite spontaneous revolt which bewildered union full-timers who had hitherto been bemoaning their members' lack of fight. More and more hospitals, inspired by the Bristol strikers, held special and unusually crowded meetings to discuss action. Union negotiators went back and managed to extract a slightly improved pay offer, only to find it threatened with inclusion in a ninety-day government pay freeze. The hospital workers' natural reluctance to withdraw their labour and concern for patient care was finally overcome with the conviction that the time was ripe to demand attention for the whole plight of the under-financed health service. One leaflet stated:

Rank and file members have at last been galvanised into action by
  (a) an abysmally low pay claim put by the official union neg-
      otiators, and
  (b) even the chance of getting this minimal claim being taken away
      by the government's imposition of a wage freeze.

An informal and unofficial rank-and-file body, the London Alliance of Stewards for Health Workers (LASH), called for a one-day stoppage on 27 November 1972, and were frankly amazed at the support it received, especially from black women workers who had hitherto been largely excluded from union activity. The strikers demonstrated for hours outside the headquarters of the Department of Health and Social Security in South London chanting 'Hospital pay makes us sick', and hooting the General Secretary of the National Union of Public Employees. The strikers' demands were radical, and they were determined, if necessary, to break the pay freeze. They called for an all-out strike for an £8 wage increase without strings, a 35-hour week, and four-week annual paid holidays. Most importantly, the mood was insistent on genuinely equal pay for women hospital workers and against productivity deals, i.e. those work-measurement bonus schemes which the hospital unions had persistently sold to their memberships in lieu of a substantial increase in the basic wage rate.

In *Backlash*, a magazine produced by LASH, was a message to the national officers:

You, people who we pay to represent us. In the past you have been doing your job in a lackadaisical way, with a couldn't-care-less attitude. Your members are now saying to you that you must get off your backsides and really do something for us. We are tired of waiting for the old pals act with management, we already know where we stand and who our friends *really* are. It's a decent living wage now or a long hard battle. Guaranteed poverty and guaranteed insecurity, that's our lot. How's life at your end, Mr Full Time Officer?[1]

The unions were forced to act if they were to retain any hold over the situation and called an official national one-day strike on 17 December 1972 which had a massive response. An estimated 180,000 went on strike, many for the full twenty-four hours. In London over 7000 took part in a demonstration to the Department of Health and Social Security and 500 attended an impromptu meeting held by the London Alliance of Stewards for Health Workers. In the North-west about 200 hospitals came out, with 2000 marching in Manchester and 1500 in Liverpool, supported by the banners of other trade unions. There was a token sit-in at the Department of Health and Social Security regional office by 150 people while a deputation took in a protest letter.

The catering staff in Oldham cut back on private patients' special meals for the duration of the action. Ancillary staff in the North-east were obstructed by management in their efforts to organise an emergency service and as a result pulled out completely in nine hospitals. Five hundred marched in Newcastle, 3000 in the Midlands, 1500 in Sheffield, a total of 5000 in Wales, and 2000 in Bristol. In Scotland 7000 workers from forty-eight Glasgow hospitals were joined on their march by striking domestic staff members from Stirling University. On the strength of this feeling, the unions began official balloting over strike action and the London Alliance of Stewards for Health Workers extended itself, for a brief period, to a national rank-and-file organisation and published a paper called *Backlash*.

By February 1973, after a complex and long-winded balloting procedure and another burst of unofficial action again led by transport union members in Bristol (who this time stayed out for four days before officials persuaded them to go back with promises of official action), national action was announced. But in contrast with the ballot's emphatic call for an all-out strike by over half the members, the unions called for a series of half-measures: selective strikes, to be co-ordinated from the head office, an overtime ban, and 'withdrawal of co-operation'. The strategy, if it existed, was to allow strong branches to take the brunt of the attack while allowing the less militant areas to choose their own tactics according to their level of confidence.

In these two weeks of March, British hospitals were shaken to their foundations. The *Concise Oxford English Dictionary* defines 'ancillary' as 'subservient' and 'subordinate'. Every ancillary worker knows what that means. Into the open came decades of quietly endured frustration: at being talked to like idiots, at watching facilities deteriorate before your eyes, at early mornings and late nights at the clock-card, at the lower depths of the lower paid. Until the strike, the vital work done by the ancillary workers was largely out of sight; in the boiler-house, the sewing rooms, the kitchens, and the record files. The general public just did not see the porter wrestling with an oxygen cylinder, the ward maid replacing blood-and urine-sodden sheets, or the hospital telephonist trying frantically to rouse doctors for a sudden case of heart seizure.

The first national strike surprised everyone, the Tories, the hospital administrators, the consultants, and many hospital workers themselves, with its determination and spirit. The picket-line posters put it plainly with the slogans 'We are against the government not the patients' and 'Hospital workers stick together'.

Women workers, scarcely represented in the union hierarchy and always blamed by male union officials for lack of militancy, led many of the strikes and marches. At one Birmingham hospital, women pickets succeeded in turning away lorry-drivers at one gate, but the latter promptly drove down the road and talked their way in through the male picket line. Workers of all languages, colours and nationalities were joined together, and signs on picket lines were in Italian, Greek, Spanish, even Gaelic. Over 400 hospitals had strikes ranging from one-day strikes to all-out stoppages. A cluster of sit-ins took place in response to management attempts to bring in volunteers. Selective action in laundries and sterilising depots began to put direct pressure on the ability of many hospitals to keep even an emergency service open, and nine hospital boards wrote to Sir Keith Joseph, the responsible Minister, asking him to pay the wage increases at once.

But as the strike dragged on, although morale stayed high where effective action was taken, financial pressure built up on the hospital workers' very small cash resources, and the mosaic-like pattern of action became confusing and demoralising. Solidarity action was hard to organise. In some cases the hospital workers had already been forced back to work by the time their industrial supporters were ready to take sympathy action. The rank-and-file organisations were engulfed, and strikers had to rely on the papers or their union full-timers, both with their own biases, or set up their own co-ordination centres, sometimes based on strike bulletins like *Flying Picket*, the Camden Public Sector Alliance *Bulletin*, or the Leeds *Hospital Worker*. Enthusiasm was replaced by frustration and tears, and when the Tories and the unions arrived at a face-saving formula, most strikers were glad to return to work. However, although the cash award was pathetic, more important points had been made – that hospital workers were no longer going to allow their dedication to be exploited and that the miracles of medicine performed by the consultants in their white coats were only possible because of a whole series of invisible, unglamorous but absolutely essential supporting workers. Without packers in the hospital sterilisation units, people to burn the rubbish, and ladies to pour the tea, even the most prestigious hospital ground to a halt. Many of the consultants who had denounced the strike action from the comfort of their limousines were to regret their remarks.

Even out of the technical defeat of the strike, a new mood of determination surfaced in the branches. For every member who disgustedly tore up his or her union card, there were a couple who rolled up their sleeves and decided to build an organisation that would be ready for the next round. Union membership swelled, especially the National Union of Public Employees, and a new national rank-and-file paper (*Hospital Worker*) was founded by a delegate conference in Birmingham and sponsored by over forty leading rank-and-file members.

In some of the militant hospitals which had gone all out for the strike and now felt betrayed individuals started the business of rebuilding the union branches. After the strike, failure though it was, things could never be the same. A new breed of hospital unionist was born. More stewards were elected, more often young, black and female. Meetings were held more often, in work time, as established in the Whitley Council rules. Joint Union Committees started up. Offices were acquired and fitted out with scrounged furniture. The issues were often little ones: grading, unjust dismissals, rest-rooms, small beer compared with national strikes. But it was necessary to recover confidence and strength for when it really mattered. One steward told me of how impressed one of the researchers in a laboratory was when the union branch asked her about some suspect and ill-packaged chemical. 'She said, "I didn't know unions did this sort of thing." You know, she'd been reading the *Mail* too much. She thought I spent all my time eating old ladies.' Another said:

After I'd wiped away the tears after the fiasco of the strike, I just went away and read the ASC Handbook from cover to cover. I found the domestics had been entitled to an extra penny-ha'penny for doing nappies. It didn't amount to much, just a bit of bunce, but it did wonders for the union.

Rank-and-file organisation

The minutes of the All London Health Workers Alliance (A. L. H. W. A.), an informal rank-and-file group formed during the strike, gives an idea of rank-and-file activities:

Solidarity action was organised for the pickets arrested at St Mary's and St George's. ALHWA delegates were sent to the demonstrations in Shrewsbury in support of the 24 building workers facing conspiracy and other serious charges because of their successful picketing during their strike.

A coach-load of people went to the founding conference of the 'Hospital Worker' paper. Five London workers were nominated and accepted by the conference as members of the editorial board. These report back to ALHWA meetings and fight for ALHWA policies and mandates on the board.

A campaign was launched to help the campaign to save Poplar Hospital. Support and £18 was given to the Portsmouth private practice strike and after to the victimised steward. A petition was printed and circulated to fight the victimisation of Bro Gibney at Hammersmith. An ALHWA contingent went on the recent march against the Lords retrospective legislation against immigrants.

Public education/discussion meetings have been held on Bonus Schemes, Problems of Foreign workers, joint shop stewards committees and TU organisation at work, Poplar Hospital and the threat of closures under NHS reorganisation, Private Practice, the 'Hospital Worker'.

Regular new and information bulletins have been sent to

workers in most of London's hospitals. £20 was given to the Nurses Action Group to start their own paper.

It was here and in the detailed hospital activities, not in the self-important but craven declarations of the union leaders, that the huge expansion of membership was achieved. It grew in little unsung battles against bonus schemes, increased canteen prices, understaffing and the use of agency and contract labour, management attempts to rationalise work and the first of the hospital closures and N.H.S. cuts.

The nurses act

The mood had altered for good. Within weeks the Nurses Action Group was leafleting nurses' homes with the message: 'Professionalism means nothing when we are used as cheap labour. We are doing a hard skilled job and we do it because we care. We also care when we are unable to do it properly because of lack of manpower and inevitable falling standards in a crumbling Health Service.' In autumn of 1973, the 1500 ambulancemen followed the defiant Scottish firemen in challenging Phase 3 of the Tory pay code, and using their traditions of militancy and high mobility they achieved a substantial increase. 'What is it worth to pick up the dead?', one poster asked starkly. The action started in Kent with a refusal to take any but emergency calls and was made national after a delegate meeting which had to be persuaded not to make an immediate all-out strike then and there. At Kent the branch secratry of NUPE reported: 'We took control of the garage to prevent any possibility of volunteers getting access to vehicles. The back door was locked, with a barricade of ambulances sideways on behind it. At the other end, we have an ambulance as a mobile barricade to let vehicles in and out.' This strength of feeling reflected not just low wages but resentment at hamfisted administration and under-appreciation of skills. Crews, for example, received no extra payment for handling over two hundred pieces of equipment in emergency vehicles.

As a North London ambulance steward wrote:

Every self-respecting ambulance man and woman wants to give what could be a wonderful rescue service. People put a lot of trust in us at a time when they are in pain or scared. We like our work and do a lot of extras from resuscitation to reassuring someone with a mental breakdown. We like the job but we have to have the bread and butter. If things go on like this many of us can't afford to do this job.

Their slogans had the same message: 'You can't eat dedication', 'No more cut-price ambulance service', and 'Our patients know our worth'. Their claim was for exactly £1 per hour, or £40 a week. Action meant only answering '999' calls into hospitals, doctors' emergency calls and urgent transfers; otherwise the men worked strictly to rule and banned overtime. In a leaflet to 'The People of London', the Joint Trade Union Conference Committee of the London Service stated:

We would like to state at the onset and with deep sincerity, that we bitterly regret we have been *forced* to resort to all-out strike action. The simple facts are that an ambulanceman's basic wage is between £23 and £26 a week, and that is by no means a living wage. And to add insult to injury, the authorities now refuse to implement an agreement which has been negotiated over a protracted period. As a result of this betrayal of our good faith, in waiting over twelve months for the results of these negotiations, we have been forced to take this drastic action in order to secure a living wage.

Nevertheless, such was the pressure being placed on the unions to uphold Phase 3 of the Tory wage restraint that NUPE, for example, withdrew its official support from the ambulancemen when only fifteen of the 140 or so areas had settled locally, which exposed those remaining out to immediate dismissal threats. The ambulancemen had shown the spark of resistance which in 1974 was to grow to a national challenge to Tory pay policy. The new Labour government dealt rapidly with the miners' strike which had precipitated the previous government's collapse. But very soon health workers were also 'special cases'.

The nurses were the first to face the new Minister, Barbara Castle. Over the previous three years, the annual wage settlements awarded by the nurses and Midwives Whitley Council had been way below the claim. In 1972, $8\frac{1}{2}$ per cent was accepted after a claim for 24 per cent. In 1973, a 40 per cent claim, the minimum necessary to keep pace with prices, resulted in a settlement of £1 plus 4 per cent. In 1972, the 55 per cent claim was shelved in favour of a 7 per cent offer before most nurses even knew that negotiations were going on. The gap between what was needed and what the working nurse actually received could not continue to widen, and in April and May 1973 the situation exploded, to the amazement of the Royal College and unions alike.

A student nurse in Leeds wrote to the *Hospital Worker*:

The militancy has sprung up very quickly. The leaders of the unions on the Whitley Council and above all the Royal College of Nursing have been caught out because they thought they had everything tied up nicely. I wrote to Alan Fisher after I heard about the nurses' settlement from someone who heard it on the radio. I asked him why there'd been no consultation with any of the nursing members of NUPE. I told him there was a new militancy among nurses. He just wrote back and said there was general fear that the government might impose a total freeze, and that it was better to get what you could rather than nothing at all.[2]

All over Britain nurses were holding spontaneous meetings, setting up informal action groups in despair of more speeches, petitions and soft soap, taking action into their own hands. The biggest single female work-force arose from its servile state with exuberance and utter disrespect for the 'right way to do things'. Birmingham nurses defied the regional NUPE secretary and his police advisers and forced their own route, two thousand strong, through the centre of the city: 'We are finished with the old image of the nurse and as such we demand a new brand of leader, not people who are too busy with their slide rules to act on our behalf.' Nine hundred nurses packed a NUPE meeting in Houldsworth Hall, Manchester, with even more unable to get in. The leaders talked, then suddenly:

a voice came from the floor demanding that Unity is Strength and we should unite with the nurses outside. This was the signal we had been waiting for. The meeting collapsed and we couldn't get out fast enough to join our fellows sat in the main road of Deansgate, holding the traffic to ransom. On reunion, the nurses surged forward on a rampage through town, banners waving, singing and chanting, under the benevolent eye of a few coppers and to the applauding hands of the public.

In Darlington nurses led the first ever march of hospital workers, joined with ancillaries, radiographers, laboratory technicians and other grades. A senior nursing officer was heard to describe the demonstrators as 'animals', but shoppers stood on the pavement and clapped while motorists sounded their horns in sympathy.

The R. C. N., who had initially accepted the March offer, now counselled silent demonstrations and mass resignations, which lay the nurses wide open to victimisation. Instead, nurses, off their own bat, were starting token strikes, restricting admissions, organising canteen boycotts, calling public demonstrations, lobbying the D. H. S. S., and contacting other trade unionists.

The higher echelons of the R. C. N. were compromised hopelessly, and although the upsurge of activity brought a wave of union recruitment, the top brass of NUPE and COHSE were slow to realise quite the extent of what was happening. A Croydon nurse wrote:

Let's be honest, all the top 'organisers' are out of the field now, dashing hither and thither – squabbling among themselves as to who is to be the one to go down in the history books of trade unionism as the champion of the nurses' cause. Let us hope that when the dust has settled it will be remembered that it was the rank and file of the nurses who led the fight for fair play with – like so many armies – the generals and the 'leaders' bringing up the rear – squabbling for their medals.[3]

More and more non-nursing unions swung behind the campaign. The convenor of the NUPE branch at St George's Hospital in London said:

Personally I'd like to see the whole movement become aware of the crisis within the NHS in the form of chronic staff shortages throughout the service, due to low pay and under-financing. At present the Press is backing the nurses – even strike action, but I wonder how they'll react when the organised trade union movement joins the press campaign and launches sympathy strikes with the nurses?[4]

For this was beginning to happen during a national day of action on 8 July. In Swansea, 1500 miners responded to the 4 a.m. flying picket of uniformed nurses and stopped the pit for twenty-four hours, and delegates from all west Wales pits called for a lodge conference to spread the action. In other areas similar moves were unsuccessful. Bristol busmen, having first voted to support the nurses' protest march demanding an independent enquiry into nurses' pay and an interim award, after some backstage manoeuvring, decided, to the disappointment of the nurses, to reverse their decision. The editorial of the *Western Daily Press* (headed 'Let light e'er shine on power, lest that power corrupt') chortled: 'Bristol busmen are to be congratulated in foiling this nihilist nonsense.'[5]

The setting up of the Halsbury Inquiry did much to damp down action, as it was intended. With their leaders having crossed the moat to the Castle, many of the early action groups, which had depended on the good will and leadership of senior nurses, floundered. Even the action groups with more union experience were unable to use their own union machinery to push new demands on their national negotiators. Nurses were still suspicious of the government inquiry. A typical leaflet of the time stated:

No Government has fulfilled its responsibility to the NHS. Our claim has been in front of the Government for two years and nine months. All we have had in that time is interim payments, percentages of next to nothing. The Halsbury Inquiry is another move to stall nurses' pay. Barbara Castle made made no real promises. There are always ifs, buts and mays. The longer we wait, the less our money is worth. We do not need an inquiry to tell us we are badly paid. We need the money now.

Indeed *The Times* reported that Lord Halsbury was at one point on the verge of suspending the inquiry because of the continuing industrial action.

When the inquiry finally reported, a total of £170 million was raised, which, as usual, was reported as '30 % average increases for nurses', although the increases varied from 58 per cent for the higher minority staff grades to as low as 5.6 per cent for first-year students over 21 years of age.

Medical technicians

In the meantime medical technicians in the Association of Scientific, Technical and Management Staffs struck and were joined shortly by hospital radiographers. Over 3000, of the country's 8000, marched in uniform through Central London on 6 July 1974, demanding an interim settlement with slogans like 'No Raise, No Rays', '30 per cent or Bust' (illustrated by an enormous bosom), 'X-Ray Pay Up Now' and 'Your Genes in our Hands'. Radiographers in the Royal Free Hospital became the first ever to strike – 'a last desperate measure to save our profession' – and they were joined by an all-region stoppage in the North-east. This led to an interim settlement averaging 22 per cent being made in the autumn and the first full review of paramedical wages for twenty-five years by Lord Halsbury, and which eventually awarded rather larger sums.

This new unity among the paramedical workers has been deepened by the work of the National Union of Students in fostering links between all health students, despite the reluctance of some medics to acknowledge the existence of the fellow members of the health team.

N. H. S. engineering workers joined the cascade. The official doctors' organisations were still adamant over private practice and the general practitioners began a campaign to refuse prescriptions for contraceptives and demote some of their registered list of N. H. S. patients, say all those whose surnames began with a designated letter, to the status of temporary patients. The letter pages of general practitioners' periodicals were buzzing with ingenious schemes to put pressure on government by refusing the numerous administrative responsibilities required of general practitioners. By the summer months most sections of the N. H. S. had taken action, including 50,000 doctors, 11,000 dentists, 370,000 nurses (who succeeded in Wales and Manchester in bringing out miners and engineers in sympathy strikes under the slogan 'Strike a blow for the nurses'), 4700 radiographers, 4500 physiotherapists, 1600 occupational therapists, 350 dieticians, 200 speech therapists, 250 remedial gymnasts, 270 orthopaedists, and 150 chiropodists. It was a strike-wave which would have seemed impossible only four years earlier, and for a period it was impossible to open a newspaper without seeing a striking hospital worker in uniform striding across it. The Halsbury Report, which was produced to settle the majority of the technical and paramedical staff's claims, was forced to award sizeable settlements, although these were highly stratified and, in fact, gave comparatively little to the junior grades.

Junior doctors

It was from this summer of hospital discontent that the Minister made her promise to the hospital junior doctors of a basic 40-hour working week. That the juniors should still be embarrassed about asking for some recognition for the hours they worked as residents indicates quite how medieval their work relations still were, although they, of all doctors, are in closest contact with other hospital workers and hospital unions. Castle's promise turned out to be empty. There would be no real reduction of hours, and overtime was to be paid at a level lower than the basic rate. Without new money it meant nothing and thLabour pay policy blocked any fresh source of finance.

The dispute which produced the first emergency-only and 24-hour stoppages by junior doctors in British hospital history between October 1975 and January 1976 was hopelessly muddled, even though the doctors' case was extremely strong. The consultants attempted, with some success, to link it up with their contract and private-practice dispute, while the establishment was fiercely behind the government's pay policy ('It must be No to the juniors. The government must not give way to the junior hospital doctors, or its £6 pay policy will be a stretcher case', wrote *The Economist*[6]). Many potential trade-union supporters were confused by loyalty to pay policy, worry about the private-practice angle and the manifest anti-socialist attitudes of some of the more noisy spokesmen of the doctors. Many senior doctors were adamantly opposed to industrial action on any grounds.

There were relatively few who were both against the £6 limit and who saw the justice of the juniors' case, although they included many of the hospital unions' branches who had been in battle over the previous year. The *Guardian*, a firm opponent of the juniors, was right in suggesting:

> there are probably two reasons why the doctors' dispute is not likely to take on the significance that the miners' strike of 1974 has in retrospect. The doctors have failed to attract the public sympathy the miners won and maintained. This is partly because the doctors have not been as clear in their aims – and their aims have been less obvious.[7]

The juniors themselves were in a state of political flux, divided in organisation, unsure of where to look for their real allies, with the old professional loyalties lingering on, although the logic of the dispute pressed them more and more towards the very trade unionism they had been brought up to fear and condemn. Yet for a growing minority, medical trade unionism is becoming both logical and attractive, and there is certainly no longer any excuse for those inside or outside medicine to assume any longer that the medical profession is automatically a preserve of reaction.

Despite themselves and their organisations' histories, hospital workers of all grades are being forced into each other's arms, and signs of this reluctant unity have been most clearly seen in a common resistance to the public expenditure cuts. In the hospitals, far from too much militancy, the problem has been not enough. Instead, conditions deteriorate remorselessly and silently, and individuals destroy themselves in attempts to overcome lack of resources with excesses of personal diligence. It has undoubtedly been the initiative of ordinary hospital workers, often at loggerheads with their official leaderships of all stripes, which has forced the politics of health care out into the open. It has brought with it an expanded conception of trade-union militancy which is not simply about wages and conditions, vital as these are as the starting-point and principles of health care. Far from letting down the patients by strike action, it has been the best advocacy of the patients' case for a health service which at last receives the finance the execution of its critical work deserves. Ironically, the frustration with the Whitley Council, 'trade unionism from above', has created a willingness to take direct action and rank-and-file initiative over general political issues, which is exactly what Whitley sought to prevent fifty years ago!

9

The cuts

By 1973 it must have seemed to the jubilant nurses who had just won their first decent pay award, to patients who were being treated in the brand new hospitals which had, at last, come into use, to the G. P.s who had begun to practise in greater numbers from custom-built health centres, that a new era was in sight. Health spending had at last increased, hospital wages were for the first time, at least for some, at a reasonable level. It has proved a mirage, a tantalising glimpse of what could be done, but not the shape of things to come. Instead, the real spending on health, in contrast to the expansion of the early 1970s, has plummetted, hacked back to 'nil-growth' by government edict, its real value sapped by inflation, manacled by cash limits, and gnawed by the price rises of its main supplies: a coalition of events collectively known as 'the cuts'. Only five years later in 1978, it is proving impossible to find the money to pay wages of the staff who were to work in the newly built hospitals which, in mockery, stand empty.

An era has ended. The public expenditure cuts mark the end of a twenty-year era in Britain in which both major parties accepted a responsibility towards the steady expansion of the N. H. S. even if the real resources were always far short of what was needed to rectify the prolonged under-financing. Now, under the impact of the world depression, both parties have undergone an overnight conversion. The cuts are a code-word for a social revolution: for a harsher, meaner, less caring Britain, for the return of the Poor Law mentality. There is a new social philosophy in the air: the welfare services, it is now agreed, are not really in existence to help human need, to heal the sick, to develop the imaginations of the young, to ease the loneliness of the old. In fact they are in existence to discourage people using them. 'The Welfare State flourished because the Growth State prospered', concluded the Centre for Studies in Social Policy: 'Social expenditure in the past has been designed to encourage customers to raise their expectations and demands. . . . In the new circumstances, it could be argued that the emphasis of policy should be to discourage additional demands.' The Welfare State is now to be judged in terms of its contribution to productive industry, which turns out to mean profit-producing industry; and judged on that basis, it is being more and more often suggested that the services are positively harmful, creating a molly-coddled indolence among citizens who are bombarded so profligately with luxuries that they are virtually prevented from finding their way to honest (profit-producing) toil.

The extent of the retreat is hard to measure with the eye, and it has led to rather bewildering re-alignments. High Tory consultants are to be heard praising the thought of Catholic radical Ivan Illich's pre-industrial utopia, health accountants wax eloquent about the bare-foot doctor pioneers in revolutionary China or the techniques of self-examination pioneered by feminist radicals sick of medical authoritarianism. The spirit of Samuel Smiles is evoked, seriously. In order to make the cuts palatable, they have been, in part, achieved under the cover of a 'redistribution' of spending, which in original conception would enjoy the support of radicals, but in practice is being used to level down spending rather than raise the standards of traditionally poorly endowed areas. Labour government advisers, after a period of denying that the cuts existed, have attempted to give them a radical gloss by claiming that the closure of hospitals is somehow an attack on medical authoritarianism and hospital overspecialisation. The very fact that this attack on public welfare has been carried out by a Labour government, traditionally supporters of public provision, and that it is a Labour Chancellor who is receiving the plaudits of businessmen, further confuses the picture. Those whose loyalty to Labour's past obscures their vision in the present are to be heard drafting plans for 'socialist' cuts, as if measures which should have been taken in the days of the boom will be taken now. A massive public-relations operation is being carried out, not by the usual and expected chorus of bankers and backwoodsmen but by traditional Leftists like Michael Foot to alter people's conception of what they are entitled to, in an endeavour to create a mood of guilt that we should ever have dared to want modern hospitals or adequate social security and to engender a mood of futile sacrifice. Healey's paternal ire at the banqueting table and Foot's trembling evocation of 'the red flame of socialist courage' are in support of a system which would have scandalised Bevan even if it would not have surprised Marx.

The economic crisis

What has been engineered in Britain in the late 1970s, and it has been deliberate rather than the result of some typhoon, hurricane, illness or other natural disaster evoked so colourfully by government Ministers, is a conscious transfer of wealth into company profits and to the owners of government loan stock away from wages and social welfare. In the words of the former Economic Editor of *The Times* who became British Ambassador in New York, 'One wonders how Ministers will feel when they realise that all their labours have merely led to a gigantic redistribution of priorities in favour of the rentier owners of gilt-edged securities.'[1]

The most senior of those ministers is only too well aware of what is happening. Denis Healey told *Business Week*:

Although I have cut expenditure in many social fields, I have been increasing expenditure in the business field. The relief I have given in tax concessions on stock appreciation is higher than any relief afforded to business anywhere in the world during a period of inflation. And very few manufacturing companies will be paying any tax at all in consequence this year.[2]

The tax ceiling for workers on the other hand, fell dramatically, meaning that, twisted by inflation, most lowly paid workers now paid tax at a uniquely heavy level, part of a general decrease in wages which led *The Economist* to comment in June 1975 that 'Britain is a cheap labour country and fast becoming cheaper.'[3]

The price of this transfer has been the deeper tax bite into weekly wages, very considerable rises in the price and the profits of the public services, very rapid general price increases, especially in food, the sharpest fall in real wages since the late 1920s and the highest unemployment since the war. It is by no means clear that the stated object of the exercise, higher investment in industry, has been attained. But it is only too evident that, already, cuts in social services, most markedly in education and health, have already permanently narrowed the range and quality of the services offered.

As we have seen, this battle between public welfare and private affluence is the oldest argument in the history of medicine. At every stage of the development of our health service, it has been denounced as economically extravagant and morally unsuitable and it has fallen to radicals to defend the budget. Those arguing for the closure of hospitals, the scrapping of services and the reduction of staff in 1978 are the spiritual heirs of the Boards of Guardians whose very parsimony made them immune to human feeling and who became numb to the untended need they witnessed daily. Like the Victorian moralists, they would never dream of allowing themselves or their relatives to endure the conditions they cheerfully inflict on others.

The computerised zombies who produce hundredweights of draft plans which seek to prove the logic of cuts which people with first-hand experience of the services know make no sense, remind one of Charles Dicken's famous character, Mr Gradgrind, the spirit of Victorian utilitarianism with its philosophy of 'Help yourself because I'm damned if I will'. They have new pocket calculators and photo-copies of draft plans but are in spirit Gradgrinds 'With a rule and a pair of scales, and the multiplication tables always in his pocket, sir, ready to weigh and measure any part of human nature, and tell you exactly what it comes to.'

N. H. S. financing

Since so much high-sounding nonsense is propagated to obscure the realities of the cuts in the health service, it is worth restating some of the home truths about the financing of the N. H. S.

- Our health spending remains markedly lower than other compara-ble countries. France and West Germany spend 1 per cent more of the national income on health services, Sweden, Canada and the United States 2 per cent or more.

- There has been a world-wide increase in the cost of medical services; but British health spending has grown from its original low levels even slower than those countries with much better existing facilities.

- There has been a persistent, chronic under-financing of the N. H. S. which all parties acknowledge but no government has been forced to remedy.

- Britain is not over-taxed, nor do the managerial classes do especially badly. Studies show the redistributive effect of sixty years of progressive taxation is not between the poor and the rich, but between the very rich and the rich. There is still a very high degree of concentration of wealth-holding in Britain in the 1970s.

- Britain has a much *lower* level of taxation than comparable countries, although it is levied principally on incomes as opposed to goods. Austria, Belgium, Canada, Denmark, France, West Germany, Holland, Norway and Sweden all have higher total taxation. Employers make a uniquely low contribution towards welfare in Britain. John Garrett, Labour M. P. for Norwich South, put it well in the House of Commons cuts debate on 9 March 1976: 'Indirect taxation in Britain is very much lower than in other European countries and has been falling relatively over the last few years. Employers' social security contributions are much lower here. Stock relief on taxation to companies will be worth £1200m. Capital allowances to companies will be worth £1800m. We are pouring buckets of money over the corporate sector without any appreciable return in terms of industrial performance or any means of monitoring that performance.'

- The first European Social Budget (1970–5) suggests that Britain's spending on 'social protection' per head of population is less than half that of West Germany, Holland and Denmark and a third lower than that of France.

- The N. H. S. takes a relatively small proportion of the total of public spending. If that money, very approximately a 'social wage' of £1000 a year per person, is subdivided, over half of it is in fact spent in the interest of the state rather than in the interest of individuals: £91 goes direct to paying interest, still including interest still being paid on money borrowed to compensate industries nationalised in 1945; also, £126 goes on defence and external relations, £112 to industry, £78 on roads and transport – and £166 is spent on the health and social services. The cuts guarantee that restrictions are *not* across the board; in fact payments to industry are increasing rapidly.

- The White Paper on Public Expenditure in England and Wales shows how health spending has plummetted locally too, here compared with spending on law and order by giving the percentage difference from the previous year.[4]

	1973–4	1974–5	1975–6	1976–7
Law and order	+4.5	+6.2	+7.3	+0.3
Health	+16.2	+9.3	+7.2	−3.7

- Far from frivolously wasting money on esoteric specialisms, the money is at present insufficient to make full use of the potential of medical knowledge which has existed for decades. We have over half a million patients with known disease waiting for surgery, a quarter of them having waited for over a year. We lie ninth in the European league table for infant mortality, perhaps the soundest single guide to the standard of general health.

- There will always be an increase in demand for medical attention as science advances what can be tackled and people become more knowledgable and demanding about their own health. The type of demand will always be altering but its quantity is bound to grow, especially as the structure of the population changes. In every study there is still evidence of reserves of unmet medical need detected. From suicide to kidney failure, there are lives which could undoubtedly be saved if the right sort of medical aid was available. For example, England and Wales may be expected to generate each year about 2000 new patients with chronic renal failure. In 1975 there was a demand for 1500 renal transplants, 5200 people on home dialysis and 2650 on hospital dialysis. All that could be provided was 542 operations, 1307 patients on home dialysis and 623 on hospital dialysis. Britain stands seventeenth in the International league table with sixty-two patients per million either on dialysis or with transplant. The Swiss equivalent per million is over twice that, 136, and Denmark, Japan and the United States all have over 125 patients per million alive and on treatment.

- N. H. S. expenditure as a proportion of over-all Government spending has declined from 15.1 per cent in 1964, to 13.75 per cent in 1973, and to 11.58 per cent in 1974.

- Illness is known to increase in times of economic hardship. The *Sunday Times* reports that 'New research at Johns Hopkins University in Baltimore suggests this startling relationship: the economy gets worse, we all get sicker. Specifically, the researchers found that about a year after unemployment increases, infant mortality rises sharply. So does heart disease (with about a two to three year time lag), cirrhosis of the liver (with about a two year lag), strokes (with a far longer seven to nine year lag), and acute mental illness resulting in hospitalisation.'

• There is positive evidence that the recognition of serious and treatable illness can be delayed by the reluctance of G. P.s to make investigations. Doctors who tell patients, particularly the old, that they have to live with a complaint, often do so as a substitute for a full diagnosis or out of ignorance of methods of treatment beyond the purely pharmaceutical. The greater the barriers, psychological or financial, put between the patient and the doctor, the longer the period which elapses before effective treatment ensues. When existing facilities close, only a proportion of the illness they dealt with will find its way to alternative facilities, and some will be 'lost', i.e. lie untreated in the community.

The New Right

Those who accept that health spending must be cut, and argue about how this should be done, have let the first stage of the argument go by default. Indeed, if we follow them we are in danger of a return to an economic consensus which pre-dates Keynes and is set on repeating the same downward spiral of unemployment, low demand, low investment and high misery of the early 1930s. There is a new viciousness abroad in social thought, perhaps best exemplified in Sir Keith Joseph and his Centre for Policy Studies, which positively attacks the 'social-democratic status quo', the Beveridge triad of full employment, high wages and the Welfare State. This view is animated by an active dislike of the collectivist approach, all forms of 'interference' and the old enemies of the eugenicist, social groups IV and V. Mainstream Tory thought is now eloquent against the feckless demands of the teeming gammas and epsilons and the social spending they are thought to require, indeed against socialists, social workers, sociology and the like.

The New Right seeks to refurbish a moral case for capitalism as explicitly as the nineteenth-century champions of *laissez-faire*, to explain and justify the virtues of self-interest, the dynamism evidenced by the ownership of wealth, the corresponding fecklessness manifest by those who insist on remaining poor. Until the mid-1970s, the Tory Party was, in the words of *The Times*'s political commentator:

to preserve the stability of society so that the existing distribution of property should be as little disturbed as possible and this was thought to require full-hearted acceptance of the welfare state and the mixed economy in the form these had been bequeathed by the Attlee government.

Now an active anti-socialist and anti-welfare policy is being toyed with, backed by the ideas of the economist Milton Friedman and the philosopher F. A. Hayek which makes the Selsdon Man seem a liberal. And it is receiving effective support, in deeds if not words with harsher cuts from the Labour Cabinet than the Tories could ever achieve and only the most feeble opposition from the Labour back-benches.

Charges for health

Throughout the early 1960s there were odd recommendations by economists and doctors for a return to the 'law of the market' in health services. They were left crying in the wind. D. S. Lees argued that 'medical care is a commodity to be bought and sold'; J. S. Searle proposed in 1962 a two-tier health service, with a major part of hospital and first-degree care on a fee-paying basis, assisted by private insurance. Even when Ivor Jones, a rotund exponent of cash-nexus medicine, submitted an official report to the B. M. A. in 1970 which suggested a split-level system with a compulsory basic rate and a 'voluntary' additional scheme 'which offers higher benefits' at higher premiums, it was still a far-fetched proposition.

The most emotionally loaded health charge, for Labour at least, was prescription charges, the issue over which Harlod Wilson himself resigned from the post-war Labour government, about the only thing most people know about this part of his career although he later stated the terms of his resignation: 'It was a practical problem. Nye saw it more as an issue of principle.' The new 1952 Tory government introduced prescription charges of one shilling a form and charges for dental treatment which raised £20 million, about 5 per cent of the N. H. S. budget. The charges were raised to one shilling per item at the end of 1956 and two shillings per item in 1961, although this represented just under a quarter of the total average cost of a prescription. The 1964 Labour government abolished the charges but reintroduced them in 1968. Like pay-beds, although the prescription charges are of trifling financial importance, they do contain a matter of principle.

The Socialist Medical Association (S. M. A.) had predicted that despite promises for exception for those in need, particularly the chronic sick, there would be immediate evidence of injustice. The S. M. A. had argued that they were unjust in application, in that they would deter people from seeking treatment to which they were legally entitled. They are also uneconomic as, out of the money raised, a large proportion would be swallowed up in administrative costs. The arrangements for exception were particularly arbitrary, and excluded, for example, those taking medicine for mental illness. One couple wrote to the S. M. A.:

> I am writing to you not to plead poverty that we cannot afford the crippling charge of 12/6d (5 items of different tablets). I am most grateful that my wife can obtain some little benefit from these tablets. My reason for writing this is to offer it as a sample case of the unfairness of the scheme for exemption of prescription charges of the chronic sick. Most of the illnesses listed under the heading are unpronounceable – most people have never heard of them, much less suffer from them, whereas the more common, but still chronic forms of illness, such as asthma, bronchitis, heart disease, etc. are not included.

Despite charges and although squeezed continuously by the costing policy of private suppliers and suffering from chronic under-financing, the small but steady growth in budget continued until the November 1973 Barber mini-budget, whose total cuts amounted to some £1350 million. The cuts were aimed at some of Labour's sacred cows: school milk, subsidised school meals, prescription charges. They were all the more galling because the Tories could claim accurately that the cuts had been pioneered by Labour, who therefore had no right to get high and mighty about their extension.

Nevertheless, in view of the relative modesty of the cuts by current standards, Labour reaction was fierce. Roy Jenkins, moving a censure motion on these 'mean and unfair' cuts, argued that they were based on 'petty dogmatism and shortsighted materialism'.

The Pharmaceutical Society stated that 'These moves are going to stop any hope we have of getting into the field of preventative medicine. Some people will become seriously ill before they go for treatment. The clock has been put back twenty years.' The nutritionist, John Yudkin, argued particularly against the increased charges for school meals and cuts in school milk, saying, 'In the past, the most important single contribution to the improvement of the diet of working class families was the provision of welfare foods, especially welfare and school milk.' Professor Peter Townsend said, 'The combined effects of the cuts in income tax in welfare will be to redistribute income from the poorest to the wealthier section of the community.'

These cuts took place in the midst of the biggest boom in British economic history. Just a week before Barber's cuts, Peter Walker, the Secretary of State for Trade and Industry, told a Young Conservative meeting that 'The years 1973 and 1974 will be noted for the beginning of sustained economic growth and for the beginning of a renewal of capitalism.'

An editorial in the *Investors' Chronicle* offered some explanation of quite how that boom was squandered:

In the summer of 1973, the government was allowing the amount of money for use in the country to expand rapidly in the hope that industry would use it to invest in new plant to produce more goods and earn more foreign exchange by exporting. It did not work out like that, because industry was not confident that it could sell enough goods profitably enough to cover the money for new plant. So the extra money being pumped into the economy found other uses. At first some of it found its way into buying shares where it helped to force prices up. More important, vast sums of money were being lent by the banking system to buy property. Since property is in limited supply, the main effect was to force prices sky high.[5]

In short, the first cuts were introduced at the peak of a festival of speculative office-building, fringe-bank fiddles and overseas 'fast-buck investment'. A particularly unpleasant aspect of the 1972–3 boom was the habit of financial experts, some of whom had profited personally from some of the shadier elements of the boom, of blaming those most innocent of any part in this unsavoury spectacle, the 'unproductive workers', the people who worked in hospitals and schools, trains, buses and post offices, for the ensuing collapse.

There is a moral ugliness, over and above the hardship caused by the financial stringencies, in this talk. It ill behoves fringe bankers, tax lawyers and company directors who have made and wasted their profits, addressing from their sumptuous offices in the socially useless office developments which have ruined so many of our towns, to talk of our understaffed schools, jerry-built council housing, museum-piece hospitals and dwindling public transport as extravagant luxuries. Wealth is produced by labour, not speculation, and labour is not yet carried out by robots. People who work in factories need to travel there, they have children who want to learn, their mums and dads are frail and need care. Even the most shortsighted of managers must realise he needs a healthy, literate work-force. One does not have to be a raving Bolshevik to see the work done by a nurse on a ward paid for out of general taxation as more worth while than the manufacture of plastic Starsky and Hutch models, even if they do create profit for an individual and can be seen as supporting the export drive.

There was quite a fierce protest against Barber's cuts. Margaret Thatcher was greeted by knots of parents and dubbed 'Thatcher – Milk Snatcher' for her contribution. Medical students in white coats marched down Harley Street with a banner asking 'Can You Afford to be Ill' and B. M. A. House was locked up lest it be set under siege. The Merthyr Tydfil Council attempted to continue to supply milk in defiance of Thatcher, arguing that its abolition was part of a 'gradual and stealthy erosion of the Welfare State'. There is little doubt that what must have seemed petty and irrelevant acts of meanness, following so closely the blatant self-aggrandisement of the boom, did much to increase support for Labour, whose manifesto reasserted 'basic socialist goals' to bring about 'a fundamental and irreversible shift in the balance of power and wealth in favour of working people and their families'. The document promised that there would be no cuts. On the contrary, 'educational expenditure will be increased, with a major priority in this sector being nursery schools'. It added firmly, 'It is clear that more money must be spent on the health service.'

Labour in office

Despite some cosmetic operations, however, which froze rents, released £350 million for housing, introduced food subsidies and increased pensions, the immediate effect of which was to be whittled away quite rapidly, they did nothing to restore the Conservative cuts. Early in the Labour government's period of office, in July 1974, medical professional associations had warned of the need for urgent cash aid to the N. H. S. In November 1974 the British Medical Association joined up with the British Dental Association, the Joint

Consultants Committee, the Royal College of Nursing and the Royal College of Midwives and published a statement on the effect financial stringency and inflation were already having on medical standards. The document they presented at the time to the Prime Minister, and which asked for an immediate injection of £500 million and a swift increase of the proportion of G. N. P. going to the N. H. S. to 6 per cent, was then seen as a piece of self-interested medical pleading. However, it was in fact a very accurate warning of the shaky state of the N. H. S. and prediction of the medical dangers further cuts would entail. It was made reluctantly:

The major health care professions have a duty to make known to Government their anxiety if and when they believe that standards and facilities are falling or have fallen below an acceptable professional level. The professions are convinced that this point has been reached.

The joint deputation went on to list a number of areas in which under-financing was in danger of causing unacceptable medical standards. They noted that the very modest targets of the Hospital Building Plan would now never be attained, remarking on 'grave deficiencies' and noting that 'Many hospitals in use today are more in tune with the old Poor Law system than with the practice of sophisticated health care of the 1970s.' They commented on the effect that the cut-back on the health-centre programme and postgraduate training in general practice was having on entry into general practice, and noted in the year ending 1 October 1973 that 93 per cent of the net increase in the number of principals was made up of migrant doctors. The dentists emphasised that the cuts had 'put on ice' interim plans on pre-ventative dentistry, emergency dental treatment – a notorious problem – the training of dental hygienists, and improvements in school dentistry. These cancelled measures might have done some-thing to avert the very rapid fall in standards in N. H. S. dentistry in the following years.

The nurses were especially concerned with ward standards, where staff shortages and the recommendations of the Salmon Report, which led to the removal of more senior nurses from the ward to administration, had worsened the situation: 'there is inadequate supervision of the unqualified by the qualified and, further, wards and departments are left in the charge of unqualified personnel to an increasing extent, particularly during the night hours'.[6] In the community the nurses cited a survey conducted by the D. H. S. S. itself of nine local authorities selected at random in October 1973, where the total D. H. S. S. recommended minimum number of health visitors was 1251, and of district nurses 1445. The numbers in post were 718 and 1212 respectively. In midwifery, the single example of the Hastings area was given. Here the requested establishment was 123, the absolute minimum numbers estimated by the midwives themselves to give safety cover were 112, the funded establishment was 96 and the numbers in post were 82.

Concerning the state of N. H. S. buildings, the report estimated that immediate maintenance work of £100 million needed to be carried out, that new buildings, at present blocked, were in urgent need if the new patterns of community health, mental health, general practice and screening which had been adopted were to have any chance of catching on. The lack of adequate maintenance, support and supply facilities, blocked for short-term economy, were forcing dependence on even more expensive commercial facilities. The presidents and deans of the Royal Colleges and the medical faculties of the universities, in a statement issued shortly after, while disagreeing with the bleakness of the B. M. A., made essentially the same diagnosis: 'The NHS has been under-financed since its inception.' They warned that 'The ills within the NHS are serious. By threatening standards, they threaten the health and wellbeing of the community.'

Public expenditure cuts

These warnings were not merely ignored. After the October election (now with a majority of three) the Labour government produced a White Paper in January 1975 which planned to level off public expenditure, chopping it by a further £900 million, of which £75 million would come from the health service. At the October 1975 Labour Party Conference, they were presented as merely slackening in the rate of growth of services, although Wilson admitted candidly that they were to be permanent: 'In the reviews we have had to make, up to five years ahead, long after the present recession has ended, we shall make sure that our expenditure is strictly related to our priorities.' The figures for the fall in spending are complicated and bedevilled by the constantly altering real value of the cash totals. What is seen easily is that the brief period of expansion of funds to the N. H. S., which had paid for the Halsbury wage round and underwritten the cluster of new hospitals and health centres in the early

1970s, had come to a grinding halt. The effect was devastating on the district general hospital building programme, the keystone of the reorganised health service, as well as on health centres, the basis of the planned renaissance of primary medicine.

In the first half of the 1970s health spending grew annually at about 4 per cent, but over 1976–7 the equivalent estimated figure is 2.7 per cent, and the projected figures for 1977–8 and 1978–9 are 0.9 per cent and 0.7 per cent respectively. This 'zero-growth' was made possible by very stringent cuts in the hospital building programme which has cancelled the long-promised and oft-postponed 300-bed 'nucleus hospitals' which were to be centrepieces of the reorganised service.

But the sudden brake on spending to nil-growth proportions greatly *underestimates* the real impact of the cuts. Wage settlements, like those awarded to the junior doctors, have to be paid out of existing funds rather than being covered by new funding from the Treasury. All figures were 'inflation-budgeted' to allow for a 10 per cent inflation rate. In fact the rise in costs of supplies to the N. H. S. was at least double, further reducing the real value of the budget. For example, not only has the number of prescriptions made out by doctors increased steadily but their cost to the service has jumped from £142 million in 1968 to an estimated £415 million in 1977. Over the same period, the average cost of an out-patient attendance in a large acute hospital increased from £2.43 to £9.20 – a jump of 378 per cent, for, far from the suppliers of the N. H. S. cutting their prices and profits, both have been increased at record rates. The already costly parts of the N. H. S. budget have gnawed even harder at the budget as the total cash allowed shrinks.

In the past central attempts at forcing economies have been thwarted by the hospitals' natural desire to spend according to need. If a particular sector of the service overspent on its planned allowance, and could show its expenditure as necessary to cope with medical needs, it would usually be compensated. Hospital authorities are notoriously careful with their budgets, so more cases of 'over-spending' were, in fact, examples of under-budgeting. But since 1969, Whitehall has been tightening control over budgets and from 1975 began operating such strict 'cash limits' that regions were effectively forced into bankruptcy if they did not make economies, regardless of the effect on medical standards. This new discipline, regardless of medical and social cost, was made possible by the 1974 N. H. S. reorganisation, a much discussed event, which like another hotly debated decision, British entry into the E. E. C., was once the hope for a new future and is now blamed for every single thing that has gone wrong.

1974 N. H. S. reorganisation

In seriousness, the 1974 reorganisation, although justified in impeccably logical terms as essential to break down the wasteful duplication of functions in the tripartite system, has had the net effect of increasing centralised control. The platitudes of American management theory, plastered over the informal and rather lethargic amateurism of British hospital administration, have produced the worst of both, a still inefficient but now faceless bureaucracy. The guiding principle of the system is that of commercial business, 'direction downward, accountability up', a good recipe for a Wall Street broker's office but not a West Midlands geriatric home. There were undoubtedly faults with the old Regional Hospital Boards and Hospital Management Committees, easily nobbled by consultants, blasé about complaints, unrepresentative of ward staff. But at least there was a fierce loyalty to particular hospitals. If remote and sometimes philanthropic in the bad sense of the word, the consultants turned up to carve the hospital turkey at Christmas, matron played tombola at the League of Friends fete, the worthies from the local Labour Party and trade unions, while seldom radical firebrands, were at least some human link between the hospital and those local people likely to use it; but then, as the team which prepared the 1974 Plan put it, in an unguarded moment, 'For our purpose, patients are not part of the organisation.'

Any vestige of local control over the decisions of finance and day-to-day running has been broken – and broken deliberately. The old do-gooders had too much sentimental loyalty, they would not let 'their' hospitals go without a damned good fight. The men who have been moved in to replace them have their experience in industry and are prepared to be hard-faced, heartless and ruthless, or 'efficient' as they like to call it. They talk of patient turnover, bed usage and staff savings, just like factory-owners, and they are prepared to be equally ruthless with their staff. In the old days the hospital secretary would know about the porter's grievances over morning coffee and put them right by lunch. Now the tyros from the District Management Team are more likely to be preparing a confidential report on the morgue attendant's Trotskyist leanings, and see 'forceful' top-down industrial relations as part of the logic of 1974. Between 1971 and 1975 the total number of administrative staff expanded by nearly one-third, from 70,396 to 91,865.

Not only has central government achieved a financial headlock over the regional and area authorities and centralised itself to merge the N. H. S. with social security and the Children's Department of the Home Office, but its local agents owe loyalty (and promotion) to the system above them and not the constituency below. A Welsh G. P. sardonically listed the first 281 appointees to the new area and regional health authorities:

> 78 are bankers, company directors, business executives, property developers and brokers; 39 are doctors; and there are 19 solicitors, six accountants, five retired Army officers, three ex-colonial governors, and 24 other professionals. Representing the sons of toil, we have six farmers (one lord and one knight), 11 shopkeepers, 10 supervisory staff, 18 full-time trade union officials, three railwaymen, one coalminer and one engineer. There are four of unstated occupation, and as most of the 53 women are listed as housewives they are difficult to classify; it seems unlikely that many of them have spent months waiting for an outpatient appointment, or spent hours waiting to see an overworked registrar, while a friend tries to cope with three children on top of her own.

In effect, all opinion which might have first-hand experience of the service as it really runs is shunted on to the Community Health Councils, those most toothless of watch-dogs, which allow great opportunity for letting off steam but have absolutely no power other than to tender advice, which can and is politely received and ignored.

Regional reallocation

A further complication in assessing the cuts, of particular importance to Londoners and Liverpudlians, is the Resources Allocation Working Party (RAWP). The RAWP proposals, officially a consultative document launched in September 1976, led to nothing short of panic in the four Thames regions, who were expected to absorb a cut, over and above the national stoppages, of £100 million. The concept of redistribution was, and is, entirely right. Indeed it was the Left who insisted on drawing attention to the inequalities in regional spending within the N. H. S. In 1971 twice as much was being spent on major building south of the River Trent than north of it. The G. P.s in the industrial north had much bigger lists and worse premises than those in the Home Counties. Oxford had twice as many psychiatrists as Leeds. London had over twice as many hospital doctors as Leicester. Even after the Crossman formula for evening out the regional allocations, the revenue allocations of 1974–5 showed that the same gap existed between the 'haves' and the 'have-nots'.

RAWP is a classic social-democratic cock-up, joint intellectual brain-child of that school of Labour Party theory which attempts to change society by redistributing it bit by bit until eventually you have socialism, and what one distinguished surgeon has called 'the computer-crazed zombies of the D. H. S. S.' What's more, between its conception and implementation the biggest economic crisis since the 1930s occurred. And as the *British Medical Journal* rightly put it, 'The fundamental objection to RAWP can be stated in one sentence; when resources are growing reallocation can be equitable, but in a period of recession it makes hardships worse.' As so many social-democratic schemes in times of crisis, it turned out to be a case of robbing an impoverished Peter to pay a broke Paul. The regions who receive money through RAWP are not getting more money, just less cuts.

The basic flaw in RAWP's method is that it takes no account of social deprivation or incidence of disease in awarding resources, simply out-of-date mortality rates. The result is a geographical explanation rather than a class one, generating the lunacy of designating areas like Tower Hamlets, Hackney and Brent as possessing more than their fair share of resources, which therefore are deemed suitable for siphoning off to East Anglia. The danger, of course, is that doctors fall to arguing about their region's score of slums rather than rejecting RAWP's levelling-down conception *en bloc*, or at least until resources start to grow again. The correspondence in the medical journals tended to fall for the trap of an interregional scrap, hook, line and stethoscope, with Brent consultants emphasising seedy bed-sits in the area (utterly unsuitable for recovery from surgery) and East Anglians retaliating with tales of damp thatches and low-paid cow-men.

It fully confirmed RAWP's work as a statistical nonsense, or, in the words of Sir Francis Avery-Jones, 'Anyone who has spent a lifetime in medicine can but marvel at the arrogance and effrontery of that particular brand of boffin who writes so much of the rubbish that emanates from the Department of Health.'[7] It also suggested that the overspent Thames regions were simply responding to a high level of disease rather than demonstrating spend-thrift habits.

A G. P. working in the 'most over-provided region', North-east Thames, noted that the closure of a local acute hospital in order to save £1 million could only worsen the unsatisfactory local waiting-lists, which 'despite continuous monitoring by the district management team' were over four months for medical, gynaecological, orthopaedic and rheumatological out-patients. He argued, 'It is better to have a reasonably adequate service available somewhere than rush into a situation which provides a service which is likely to be totally inadequate.' Another London physician, labouring under cuts

> which will decimate services, particularly in the acute specialities, without producing true economies [thought] transferring money from one region to another on statistical grounds may not help the recipient if the money is inadequate in quantity and badly and hurriedly spent, but it will certainly harm the donor region unless there has been gross overspending and wastage of resources.

A medical student reminded readers that all was not over-provided roses even in the prestige London teaching hospitals: 'At St Mary's our department of obstetrics and gynaecology and the school of nursing are housed in converted stables that used to belong to Paddington station, and our department of general practice is located in a building on the premises of a second-hand car dealer.' Figures cited by a correspondent from East Anglia, prime example of a deprived region, confirmed that there was a gross maldistribution according to class rather than geography within the region. Cambridge health district, with an unusually high upper-middle-class proportion of inhabitants, took the elephant's share of the budget and spent six times as much per head of population than the more solidly proletarian town of Great Yarmouth.

RAWP undoubtedly did once embody a serious claim for medical justice but has turned out just one more formula for justifying the cuts. Its first victims, Liverpool and Inner London, have a no-toriously high incidence of disease and social deprivation. What started as a great levelling has ended with those that have the least having the most taken away from them. It is worth noting that, according to Robert Maxwell's estimates in *Health Care, the Growing Dilemma*, it would only take another 0.2 per cent of the nation's

G. N. P. to even *up* all the regional differences. It is also worth bearing in mind that in Scotland, with its traditionally higher standards of medical care, an average of 25 per cent more is spent per person, which ought once again to indicate the need for a massive over-all increase in all British regional spending.

Staffing

The first, and best disguised, cuts have been achieved by freezing existing, inadequate staffing levels. The negotiated establishment for a ward or department has been concealed or replaced with an 'in post' estimation. Long-advertised consultant posts, especially in the less popular and more socially useful specialities, have been abandoned quietly. Managements were generally successful at pressing people to cover up, even though the strain of being constantly understaffed and depending on poorly trained staff in any sort of hospital work is both nerve-racking for the staff and dangerous for the patient. Further wage savings have been made by hastening the departure of staff, especially those over retirement age, by fair means or foul and seeking to cut back on the guaranteed overtime which alone makes hospital wages possible to live on. Further shedding of staff is achieved by centralisation of catering, laundry and laboratory facilities, forced through despite the inevitable decline in efficiency.

It is hard for people who have not worked in the N. H. S. to appreciate quite what a difference staff shortages can make. Yet those of us in it have become so habituated to them, to make a fuss now seems self-interested.It is not just the extra work-load but the now lost possibility of acting like a human being to another, rather than as clock-watching automatons processing people called 'patients'. That brief but reassuring chat between the ward auxiliary and shaved and dazed patient waiting to go into theatre, the spare moments for a nurse to talk to a patient who never gets people to visit him, the chance for a junior doctor to really explain what an operation entails before a signal pulls him off to some new crisis, warm ward meals, individual rehabilitation, proper training – in short, the human touch – require time and staff. Another pair of hands can really alter the whole atmosphere in a ward, department or surgery. Staffing makes all the difference but it is the first place to make economies.

In a diary of a geriatric nurse, nights with full quota of staff are recorded as making possible good patient care, but when only one night nurse is on duty the same ward is full of 'distressed, incontinent, uncomfortable patients'. On another night 'Shortage of staff resulted in cold food for those who had to be fed. A patient was left in a wet bed for 45 minutes for the same reason.'

Three doctors in the Royal Free Hospital, at its old Grays Inn Road site, reported:

On going on duty in the morning, the doctors found that although patients in the ward for acutely ill women should have been resting, some were in fact making beds. They found that the only nursing staff present were an agency SEN and a first year student nurse. The agency nurse had started at the hospital only the previous day. They found that urine samples taken during the night had been thrown away 'through no real fault of the nurses on duty, who could not be expected to know better'. And they found that patients who should have been sent to clinics were still in the ward because nobody knew that they were meant to go. In short, there was a chaotic state of affairs. The situation may have been partly caused by staff sickness, but it is merely an extreme example of what is happening every day and in all the medical wards in which we have patients.

One of the three doctors concerned said: 'It is no good saying that this isn't news, that it goes on everywhere – we know that. What we are saying is that it shouldn't. It would have been quite inconceivable for a first year student nurse to be alone on night duty in an acute ward even when I was a student less than ten years ago.'

In a report on Brookwood Hospital, in 1976 not 1946, the picture is not much better than before the era of mental-health reform:

The room is locked. The charge nurse, a youthful Oriental, says it is 'to stop them wandering'. The room is long, drab, low-ceilinged. It is cold and smells of urine. Along the sides and down the middle are rows of steel-framed armchairs. An enormous television set is turned up loud; racehorses, unaccountably sundrenched, flicker across the screen. No one is watching. There are about twenty patients in the room, all men, all elderly. Most sit slumped and empty like disregarded piles of shabby clothing.

The divisional nursing officer states the problem:

The standard of nursing care we provide here is inadequate. We have 430 nurses to look after 1080 patients, 90% of whom are classified as long-stay. 130 of the nurses are students who spend 40% of their time on courses. We should have 800. Then we could concentrate on developing community care to prevent patients becoming long-stay.

In November 1975 COHSE warned the government that staffing levels were in danger of becoming hazardous for the patients, with several branches reporting cuts in nursing overtime, extra work by nurses to cover economies made on domestic staff, non-replacement and replacement by unqualified staff. New trained nurses were needed desperately. *Four days later, Mr Eric Deakins, in a written answer to Parliament, said that the latest Department of Employment figures showed that there were 3276 qualified nurses registered as unemployed in England.*

The small hospital: Poplar and the Elizabeth Garrett Anderson

This imprisoning of hospitals through overworked and understaffed levels has been worsened by the spate of closures of small hospitals. As measured on the computer these units are not economic, but they have provided a homely atmosphere and convenient access, which is important for immobile out-patients and visitors, and various specialist facilities. Indeed Roland Moyle, Minister of State at the D. H. S. S., told Parliament: 'I think the homely atmosphere of a small hospital is no less important – it may indeed be more important – in urban community hospitals than in a rural community hospital.' Yet his department has systematically closed over 100 hospitals in the period 1975–7.

One of the first to go was Poplar Hospital, a stately if gaunt dockland hospital, which stands sentry on the East India Dock Road and served the docks of Millwall and the people of Poplar during the heaviest nights of the Blitz. Poplar had only eighty-one beds but it provided a casualty service to thousands of heavy industrial workers on the Isle of Dogs and around the docks. From the staff canteen in the hospital, you could see the dog-men on the crane hooks, tiny boilersuited figures in the electrical generator station, the ship-repair yard and dry docks, and the procession of tower blocks sloping towards Essex. This, if anywhere, was the place for a hospital; the community had served up its burns, fractures, sprains and closing-time fights to Poplar Hospital for generations. The staff at Poplar were horrified by the steady run-down of their hospital and asked 'for a cast-iron guarantee that our hospital be kept fully open. If Poplar closes we lose more than our jobs. The East End loses a hospital which has given good service for years. And the way is opened for shutting down all the small East End hospitals.'

The staff petitioned till they were blue in the face, passed out leaflets and stuck stickers and posters all over the local pubs and streets. They blocked a pedestrian crossing on the East India Dock Road by constantly crossing to and fro. They called special delegate meetings with pledges from the bus garages, docks, and tenants' associations to prepare to strike. They leafletted twenty-five other hospitals with the aid of the All London Health Workers Alliance and together went to invade the headquarters of the Regional Health Board to demand an explanation. They held marches with heart-felt and heart-rending banners and hand-made carnations. The local M.P.s made it their business to turn up and be photographed at the head of the march; but they could never apply enough pressure to the right place in the new health bureaucracy. Other hospitals were sympathetic but, wrongly, did not see it as their problem. The women ancillary workers at Poplar who led the fight combed the Isle of Dogs for industrial support, barging into rag-trade sweat-shops and making fiery speeches to Sikh pattern checkers, addressing railwaymen from a table in a canteen plastered with pin-ups, talking their way past the dock police who make entry and exit to the West India Dock more like Colditz.

Somehow, despite the promises, the support never really showed up in one place at the same time. It was murmured that perhaps people did not really like the hospital so much because so many of the doctors were foreign. One by one the facilities froze up. The consultants were bribed away with promises of improved facilities in nearby hospitals. Other small hospitals in East London *were* closed. Now Poplar is a shell, patrolled by guard-dogs.

A very similar train of events was started at the Elizabeth Garrett Anderson (E. G. A.) hospital in Euston, founded by the first women to attain, after a considerable battle against male prejudice, medical registration. Dr Wendy Love of the hospital's medical committee described the early stages in December 1974:

Three years ago the excellent nurse training school at the Elizabeth Garrett Anderson Hospital was combined with schools of the other hospitals in the North London Group as a result of Salmon. At its last inspection in November 1973 the Elizabeth Garrett Anderson compared favourably with other hospitals in the group. Meanwhile, as a result of NHS reorganization this hospital has found itself in a different District. In September we noticed from the nurses' advance change list that the supply of student nurses from the combined training school was being phased out. A formal statement was eventually issued by the district administrator explaining that the area health authority had accepted a decision of the General Nursing Council to withdraw approval of the Elizabeth Garrett Anderson for the training of student nurses. It follows that the hospital will have to rely in the future on trained or agency nurses and will become uneconomic.

Our obstetric unit at Hampstead will be closed shortly when the new 60-bedded unit opens at the Royal Free Hospital. Unless its patients can be moved to our main hospital at Euston there will be no unit north of the Thames at which women can be certain of being treated by women. We have repeatedly recommended this move to the authorities and we have emphasised the anomalous position of a women's hospital without an obstetric unit. Meanwhile, reports attributed to district and area officials have appeared in the press to the effect that the unit's patients are to be moved to the Royal Free. We have been besieged by patients complaining that their wishes are not being respected and the staff have not yet even been consulted about the transfer, which could lead to redundancies.

Two years ago Rosa Morison House, endowed as our pre-convalescent home before the NHS, was closed down at only three weeks' notice and tranferred to another hospital group. It has remained empty ever since. Our ENT [ear, nose and throat] department has been closed. For some time we have not been allowed to have our vacant consultant posts advertised and can fill them only by locums. The purpose of this letter is to alert staff at other hospitals to the steps which can be taken to make the closure of a hospital inevitable by making it uneconomic.

The E. G. A. did *not* go the way of Poplar, although for the first eighteen months the campaign followed the same path of petitions, lobbying of community health councils, area health authorities, M. P.s and councillors, where, as is the nature of these things, the talking is done by those few who are deemed 'articulate'. But although these are all vital ways of getting a campaign started, they can only go so far. It took the initiative of the NUPE chairman from the neighbouring branch to suggest to the E. G. A. unions that they start the first hospital occupation.

From that point enthusiasm grew in leaps and bounds. Supporters showed they cared by giving a regular stint on the picket line which watched the hospital twenty-four hours a day. If the authorities attempted a moonlight flit, over a hundred people could be summoned through the telephone tree operated from the hospital switchboard. Ambulance unions were able to give a positive promise not to move the patients without the occupation committee giving its approval. The staff had something new to say when they went out to meetings called about the cuts – not just 'We need your support' and 'Isn't it terrible', but now 'We are doing something, what are you going to do?' Vera Wagstaff, who seldom spoke even at union division meetings, found herself addressing rallies, meetings and trade-union committees. The ordinary members of the union, and many people who had been non- or even anti-union, found themselves arguing the case. When a speaker was needed at a meeting in East London, the occupation committee arranged, not for a 'name' but for a West Indian E. G. A. cleaner who lived out that way to speak, and an excellent job she did. Sympathisers in other hospitals where the cuts were still more intangible took up the E. G. A.'s cause and got official union backing at divisional and area level, a promise of strike support without which the occupation would have been a mere gesture.

Women's liberation supporters, who saw the hospital as a symbol of women's historical battle against the masculine dominance of medicine, took a particular and lasting interest. Local community, tenants' and pensioners' organisations took the E. G. A. as a symbol of all the other facilities taken away from them in the area, one pensioner saying, 'The NHS does not belong to the Area Health Authorities or those in Whitehall. It is our health service and unless we fight for it we will lose it.'

Outside the hospital, a banner lettered with cycle-handlebar tape said 'EGA stays OK', and another 'We are still open for the treatment of women by women'. A colour film was made of the case for the hospital, and a slide show which showed how the occupation was arranged, aimed at other hospital workers, went the rounds. The porter's office became a veritable library of radical literature. Everyone from Dame Josephine Barnes to the domestic insisted, as was stamped in red on all doctors' referral letters from the hospital, 'Treatment for women by women'.

The authorities, who had been able to wear down and demoralise even the vigorous East Londoners, were blocked at the E. G. A. Services were kept going, plans to improve them debated, local and national support was so strong that they have been unable to move in for the kill. Now in some respects, the E. G. A. is a rather special example because the good will of the senior medical staff, essential if the 'work-in' is to work, has been retained· because there is no precisely equivalent N. H. S. work in their specialised 'women treating women' field. In other hospitals, unless new forms are found of organising the medical work, say as a G. P.-run community hospital, consultants could be offered, and accept, alternative beds in remaining hospitals, and without them the work-in would collapse.

The extent of support for the E. G. A. was massive and this was possible because the hospital staff realised they were both a symptom of the threatened programme of London hospital closures, and a proof that active resistance was possible. You could cynically put it down to North London radical chic or more accurately to the deep feelings a hospital closure conjures up. But either way, the campaign had an improvised versality and fluency about it which proved unstoppable. Anarchists printed leaflets, *cinéastes* made films, G. P.s stuck up posters in their surgeries, beautifully silk-screened by the local print workshop. E. G. A. badges first sported on radical lapels were soon spotted in the street markets and at the bus stops of North London. Volunteers of all political persuasions and of none manned (and womanned) the picket rota. Hundreds of local residents volunteered their telephone numbers to become the branches of a telephone tree which could summon an instant picket to block any lightning strike by the authorities. The hospital unions were forced by a determined membership to give official backing and practical support to the E. G. A., not just the usual hot air at conferences. A caravan from the Women's National Cancer Control Campaign parked outside the hospital giving cervical smears to hundreds of women and showing the need for the Well Woman Screening Clinic which the Campaign wanted to see developed at the Euston site.

On 6 February 1978 the Camden and Islington Area Health Authority finally agreed not to force the unwanted move to the Whittington Hospital because of the 'almost universal opposition' – the decision the E. G. A. staff and supporters had been demanding for two years. In effect, they washed their hands of the E. G. A., and passed the final decision to David Ennals, the Secretary of State. In the words of the *EGA News*:

> Mr Ennals now has to find the money to fund the EGA, or face the wrath of the trade union and labour movement in the area, and women all over the country who have supported the EGA's fight for better health provision for women, and against cuts in facilities or jobs in the NHS.

Now instead of grudging acceptance of their existence the campaign wants a new commitment to the principles which animated the E. G. A.'s founders. Not just the repair of the rusty old lift but the development of a growing hospital shaped itself to answer to the real needs of the women in the area.

Hounslow Hospital was a smaller and still more neglected hospital in industrial North West London. Overshadowed by the West Middlesex and the Hammersmith, poorly serviced, badly administered, it was the obvious target for a district management team which entered 1976–7 'over-spent' – that is, underfinanced – to the extent of £500,000, and with a potential RAWP-tax of £13m. lost revenue to the Area Health Authority as a whole. The accident and emergency department, which saw 6000 visitors a year and the outpatients– 12,000 customers – were closed simply to save money. Despite this the 66 medical and surgical beds with excellent physiotherapy back-up and a devoted nursing staff would have provided, all agreed, an ideal base for a G. P.-run community hospital. As Russell Kerr, the M. P. for Hounslow, Feltham and Heston, put it:

> I want to see Hounslow Hospital defended against those who would close it on alleged economic grounds and I want to see it made into a proper Community Hospital. I reject the economic grounds being put forward for its closure by largely faceless bureaucrats . . . I'm giving my full support to those locally who have the guts and the imagination to challenge the Department's assessment of our health needs in Hounslow – and who will, I predict, earn and deserve the gratitude of Hounslow people in the years that lie ahead.

The district management team agreed on a community hospital, 'some time in the future', the Community Health Council said 'soonest', the hospital staff said 'now' and believed that 'once closed, Hounslow will never reopen'.

To ensure that Hounslow stayed open as a community hospital serving local needs, the staff decided to embark on a work-in on 28 March 1977. They stated:

In occupying Hounslow Hospital by 'working-in' we are not taking away from the Area Health Authority the responsibility they have in law for the patients and staff at our hospital. We will, however, take no part in staff transfers, closure of beds, refusing admissions or any other activity that leads to the run-down of work at our hospital. We offer assurances to the Community Health Council, the public, and in particular outpatients, that patient care will in no way be impaired, and indeed where possible will be improved. We wish to make clear that it is our intention to continue to provide patient services to those who need them and will draw support from any source where it can be obtained.

The second-ever occupation of a hospital was under way, beginning the same painstaking, patient task of building up local lines of support and an atmosphere of trust, overshadowed all the time by the authorities' death sentence. And they obtained not only 30,000 petition signatures but the practical support of the doctors, the ambulance service, their trade unions, local councillors, and the local M. P. But on Thursday 6 October 1977, the administration decided to put a stop to this. In what was described as a 'Gestapo-type raid', they hired a fleet of private ambulances and carted the patients to the West Middlesex Hospital. Many patients were distressed and shocked. Many were old; three were over 90. But that did not bother the Area Health Authority, for the hospital occupation had to be broken at all costs. Not content with this, they broke up the beds with hammers, removed the springs, threw mattresses and furniture around, to leave the hospital in a very sorry mess.

The terrified patients were given no medical examination before their kidnap, even though one patient was complaining of chest pain throughout. In the previous week a patient who was prevented from admission to a waiting medical bed at Hounslow and sent by minicab to West Middlesex Hospital, where there was no bed except in the psychiatric ward, had died.

The sickening sense of shock and disbelief was expressed by the eye-witnesses. Nurse Bernadette O'Donnell said:

The patients were not even allowed to put on their dressing gowns. There was no regard for their welfare.

Ron Keating, Assistant General Secretary of NUPE, who visited Hounslow immediately, said:

Two wards looked like a battle-ground, with beds dismantled and bedding strewn about the floor, half-prepared food lying around, some of it half-eaten, urine bottles part-full on the floor, a patient's case notes on the top of a locker. The hospital looked as if it had been invaded by the Gestapo.

Sister Stella Roe described the raid:

Old ladies had to queue up for an hour, crying all the time as we remonstrated with the area health authority people to cover them up against the cold. The nurses went back to the wards and just broke down and cried. They hadn't told me about the move — either as a nurse or a relative of a patient.

Sister Cynthia Scott, who was on duty when the officials arrived at the hospital door, said simply: 'There is no hospital left. They have destroyed it.'

Staff invited the public to inspect the damages caused by management representatives in the last harrowing scenes, touring the streets with bill-boards saying starkly: 'Your hospital has been "wrecked" COME AND SEE'.

The effect on local supporters of the campaign was profound. Stan Hunt from the nearby West London Hospital told an emergency meeting of 90 shop stewards from 34 London hospitals, convened jointly by *Hospital Worker*, the E. G. A. Campaign and CLASH, of his own feelings.

We have been down to the Hounslow work-in several times. It was always peaceful. We'd have a joke. Then this happened. What was on the T. V. was bad enough. But when me and the stewards went down, well, it shook us. We had a good look. The whole place had been turned upside down. The nurses who witnessed it were still in a state of shock. It's hard to put it in words. Now, some people might say, oh well, it's all right, maybe, if they've got alternative beds ready. But they hadn't. The patients they kidnapped from

Hounslow went into makeshift beds in the corridors and the middle of wards.

After seeing the mess, we went straight back to the members and recommended open-ended strike action from Wednesday until they reopen that hospital. We have to strike while the iron's hot. If we wait for some government inquiry, we're dead.

Hospital workers have got to start it themselves and then call on other workers to back them.

Hospital Worker caught the intensity of the bitterness by issuing a 'Wanted' poster of the Chairman of the Area Health Authority. The charges included 'Conspiracy to Kidnap', 'Disturbing the Peace of Sick People', 'Attempted Murder', 'Causing an Affray', 'Wilful Damage to NHS Property' and 'Having No Heart'.

The wave of anger washed through the London hospitals and over 3000 people beseiged the afternoon meeting of the Area Health Authority on 12 October. As the Authority hid its wounds inside the Town Hall, banners and placards draped the enclosed front entrance and speaker after speaker mounted the concrete steps to denounce the conspirators within. Middle-aged gentlemen from NALGO, jiving NUPE cooks from Hammersmith, solid determined bodies from the West London hospitals, large delegations from hospitals like the Royal Free and Charing Cross, which had held emergency meetings, smaller but vitally important knots of stewards from local industry like the massive Heathrow Airport complex and the Park Royal railway repair yards who, although not immediately affected, had risked their jobs to show their solidarity; all were there. On the suggestion of John Deason, Secretary of the Right To Work Campaign, the protesters marched down to Hammersmith Broadway to spread the word, rather than simply await the verdict. But the cars went on whizzing past above, on the flyover.

For in truth, people still did not want to know. To win a future for Hounslow would only have cost peanuts in financial terms but required politically a change of policy at Cabinet level. Try as we did, there was not yet the degree of awareness and confidence required to force a change of national policy. The 'Social Contract' had done its numbing work. Ennals stood his ground, effectively condoning an action many suspected him of having authorised in the first place. The Fleet Street print workers, the airport maintenance staff had their hearts in the right place but their fists were still in their pockets. The stewards confided: 'It's hard enough to get them out for themselves nowadays, let alone for you lot'. To those who argued and tried, thanks. The fire will come next time.

And in the meantime the Hounslow Occupation Committee, out of the ashes of its defeat, had the bravery to continue the fight by calling all-London conferences against the cuts and issuing a 'broadsheet of resistance', *Fightback*, which linked hospital occupation committees. In the first week of November they went 'on tour' to speak to hospital workers outside London about their campaign, trying to spread their experience and learn from others about how to fight against cuts and closures more effectively.

Meanwhile at the Plaistow Maternity, in the Newham District of East London, which was experiencing especially severe cuts, another work-in started on 15 July 1977. In an interview with *Women's Voice* Dot Potter, Pat Varney and Elsie Brooks explained the reasoning behind London's third work-in:

We started the occupation because it was the only answer. Something has to be done to save this small service we have in Newham. If this hospital goes, others will as well. Other closures are already planned. We live here, we've had kids in this hospital, we want to save the hospital for the people who live in Newham.

It's not as if the hospital isn't being used – it's 75 per cent full all the time. The NUPE members in the hospital set up an Action Committee and COHSE and NALGO members joined the Committee as they voted to join the work-in.

Now the Action Committee has 15 members and represents all the workers in the hospital. We've had union backing all the way, but we came to a 'mutual' agreement with the officials that we were better off without them.

We're a workers' committee, not a union committee, that stops us being divided. Practically everyone in the hospital has joined a union since the work-in started, particularly the nurses, and the union groups are much more active.

When we started the work-in, we decided certain people would have to be kept out. We've excluded our immediate bosses in the hospital, the District Management Team, and members of the Area Health Authority and the Regional Health Authority.

We felt we needed control over what happens in the hospital, and it would make us weaker if we let them in. Not many of them come in anyway, but there may come a time when they will want to, and we want to be in a position where they have to be invited in. The hospital is running as smoothly as ever, perhaps even more so. We've proved we can do without the people at the top. They expect us to fall on our faces, but we've surprised them. We're expecting a closure date before the end of the year, but the more threats the administration makes, the more determined the staff are to fight back.

We are trying to spread the campaign. We want everyone in the borough to join the fight. We need two maternity hospitals in Newham. The government and their hatchetmen have got their priorities wrong. They give us facts and figures and they overlook people's needs.

Forest Gate is tucked away in one corner of the borough. How can a mum seven months pregnant be expected to get to ante-natal clinics? Are they likely to travel three miles across the borough, changing buses on the way? They just won't be able to do it.

There are no buses to Forest Gate on Sundays and public holidays. But the Minister for Health doesn't travel on buses, so he doesn't know that. They say there's no money, but you can't weigh up lives in terms of money. We're running a service, not a business. We're just a pawn in the economists' devious game. They've chosen hospitals to cut back on, rather than other things, because they think we are less likely to go on strike.

They expect hospital workers to keep quiet – we've never fought back before. But this time we've given them a shock. We've learnt from the failure of the Poplar Hospital Campaign, and we've had help and advice from the EGA and the Hounslow campaigns. Now we need to get together and draw up a blue print to fight all hospital closures. We are determined that all of them are going to stay open.[8]

The unsung closures

For the two or three hospitals that have resisted, there are already over 100 gone since the cuts began, and probably a further total of 500 under threat; the current plans require the purging of the 185 hospitals in the six Inner London boroughs, hospitals which embody over a century of specialised medical experience and acknowledged excellence, to a mere twenty centres. As the E. G. A. campaigners put it:

The attempts to close the EGA are part of the policy of massive cuts in social services spending. 120 hospitals are threatened in London alone, and the new plans for the Camden and Islington area would cut the number of acute speciality beds by half. Small local hospitals are being singled out. They call it 'rationalisation' – but they are not spending any money to build new hospitals, so what it means to us is longer waiting lists, further to travel, more unemployment, and overall a worse standard of health care in the NHS. We can't let this happen!

D. H. S. S. policy anticipates 'the eventual closure of most if not all existing single speciality hospitals. The redeployment of hospital services and the reduction in total numbers of beds should allow a major programme of hospital closures and disposal of sites.' *But the district hospital network planned to take over was halted at the drawing-board stage.*

Ordering the closure of hospitals has been reduced to a six-month process. By the time a closure is announced, neglected maintenance, 'discovered' structural faults, withdrawal of training recognition and 'temporary' closures mean there is little worth closing. The seediness of hospital premises have made them health risks in their own right: the operating theatre in Queen Mary Hospital, Roehampton, is so old that cross-infection was found to be a danger in February 1977. In April 1976 a senior consultant anaesthetist walked out of Holloway's Royal Northern Hospital because of 'intolerable' and 'filthy' conditions in the operating theatres. A recent survey of 24,000 N. H. S. medical laboratories found 'highly variable' safety standards with poor use of protective clothing, open use of known and suspected cancer-causing substances and an 'extremely lax' safety routine.

The Rossendale Hospital in Lancashire, 105 years old, where nine women died of exposure in mid-winter, was described by the official inquiry as having 'one wall dripping with damp, with no curtains or carpets, the windows did not fit and the old people might as well have been in the open air'. Subsequently there has been a series of fires in old people's homes, with six dying in Hull's Wensley Lodge Home, eighteen in Fairfield, Nottinghamshire, two in a Bournemouth home in September 1974 (shortly after it has been recommended for closure because of fire risk). Other fires killed a nurse and two patients in a private home in Herne Hill, gutted a geriatric ward in North-west London, killing a man, and severely damaged the purpose-built Fox Hatch home in Brentwood. Even the brand new Liverpool Teaching Hospital is beset with dire fire risks, the removal of which cost several *million* pounds and was subsequently investigated by the House of Commons public accounts committee. After several years of knowingly letting people work and live in these conditions, they suddenly become a convenient excuse for closure.

If hospital workers love their hospitals, and we do, it is that ambiguous kind of love Londoners had for the wartime tube-station shelters; an affection for how well the human spirit can overcome the shabbiest of surroundings. The decades of neglect, the years of 'making do' sustained only by the promise of brand new hospitals in the near future, provide perfect victims for the predators of the D. H. S. S. Staff are often demoralised, confused by false promises, disheartened by rumours and, worst of all, somehow made ashamed of their existing equipment, their experience, their training, their pattern of working – yes, their own feelings of affection towards the people who have used the hospitals. All this falls victim to the paper projections and calculations, the airy promises of the administrators which are, at crucial points, non-specific and unguaranteed. Administrators who blithely redirect chronic patients with bronchitis or arthritis to new premises thought to be 'an easy journey' away have clearly assumed that that journey is by a comfortable car, not puffing and heaving on sometimes unavailable public transport.

Very many of these hospitals, small and perhaps economically inefficient on computer calculations, have particular qualities, cherished by those with first-hand experience. The Paddington Day Hospital was supported by fifty-two local G. P.s, who 'felt strongly that the local hospitals may be unaware of the services we need and which they are not providing', and argued, in open criticism of the proposed psychiatric alternatives, that 'a large number of our patients are not suitable for drug treatment – these are treated almost cavalierly by the physically orientated psychiatric clinics and return to our surgeries "labelled" inadequate personalities'. The visiting medical officer of St Faith's epileptic colony who stated the case for patients 'who collectively cannot speak on their behalf' had 'worked with them and attempted to help them for twenty-five years'. This unique centre for 3000 seriously afflicted epileptics is recommended for closure and its patients destined for resorting into the psychiatric hospitals and subnormality homes which have already proved wanting and unsuitable for their care. As is often the case, an excellent and humane government report *People with Epilepsy* is on the stocks with fifty-six recommendations, including the establishment of specialised units. Very few have been implemented. As the doctor comments, 'It is irresponsible to run down hospitals and close them before the perhaps utopian alternatives devised by Reid and his colleagues have yet begun to be implemented.' St Faith's has become a financial embarrassment. The severe epileptics, with their gawky movements, guarded speech slurred by continuous drug treatment and still unpredictably flying into rages and fits, are an embarrassment too.

St Wulstan's Rehabilitation Hospital in Malvern was only established in 1961 as a unique centre of industrial therapy for 1200 long-term schizophrenic patients. Its work does not consist of underpaid, off-hand, repetitive tasks landed on many psychiatric patients for the convenience of the staff, but a genuine attempt to make productive labour part of mental recovery, using pioneering community psychiatric methods. The results have been most impressive: four out of ten patients have returned to live in the community, the same patients who had, on average, ten years' stay and ten years' prolonged failure under conventional asylum regimes.

The National Schizophrenia Fellowship regards it as a model hospital and advocates that every hospital region in Britain should have a unit like it. Donel Early, an international expert on industrial therapy, states that 'Everyone knows that within the hospital service facilities similar to St Wulstan's do not exist.' Everyone, it would seem, knows except the West Midlands Regional Health Authority, who, absurdly, have convinced themselves that 'the kind of work done at St. Wulstan's is now common in mental hospitals all over the region' — would that it were. A patient wrote:

> Why must it be? Why must it be?
> Why must St Wulstan close?
> Three long years have I lingered here,
> Learning the tricks that mean survival
> In the hard outside world.
> And yet some say we are out of date,
> Wanting us back to a rat's life, in large homes.
> Lining up in queues for tablets
> Are the folks of St Wulstan's
> Heads down they expect the worst — closure,
> Heroism and dedication
> All pass before the pens of bureaucrats.
> The men and women who made St Wulstan's unique
> Will go to somewhere far less able.

There are countless others with their special qualities: the London Jewish's traditional links with East London Jewry, Brentwood Hospital's highly successful G. P. unit, Bexley Maternity Hospital's geographical convenience, the Metropolitan's distinguished and still solid buildings which have served Hackney for 110 years, the Charing Cross Drug Dependency Unit, which pioneered treatment for young addicts, Lansdowne Hospital in Cardiff, Leith Hospital in Edinburgh, Maidenhead General, Walsall Maternity. The list goes on and on, even though the cuts have *so far* been spread very unevenly and some areas have yet to experience the cuts now 'coming on stream'.

Add to this the planned facilities which will now never materialise and the full size of the problem emerges. For these long-promised new facilities, scheduled as part of a comprehensive plan and 'just around the corner' for the last two decades have now been officially abandoned. Rebuilding of the Sheffield Northern General Hospital, St Mary's Paddington, The Royal Postgraduate Medical School in London, all hospitals doing work respected world wide, is now postponed indefinitely. Areas where a rapidly expanding population has pushed existing older facilities beyond the limits, areas such as Hemel Hempstead, have been told the long-awaited new hospitals have been officially scrapped. Many hospitals have been and gone in the planners' log book without the public ever knowing.

The remaining hospitals

Neither the new resources so badly needed nor the pattern of care the existing small hospitals have provided can be squeezed out of the already overburdened larger hospitals. Instead it becomes harder to get into hospital, patients have to be more sick than before, more ill people who would have been admitted to hospital have to stay at home. Waiting-lists mount up (they jumped from 519,552 to 583,851 from September 1975 to March 1976, an increase of 10,000 a month). Patients are called in at short notice – on 'stand-by' rather than schedule – patients are discharged earlier than usual and before complications can be detected or treated successfully. Inevitably, in the remaining hospitals it becomes harder to see a specialist. There are fewer sessions, longer waits, more pressure on beds. Increasingly accident and emergency units come under medical siege from patients who are sent directly by G. P.s who despair of getting a hospital appointment in reasonable time. A casualty officer's job becomes more and more like a receiving officer under the old Poor Law. He has to balance a medical assessment against the patient's home circumstances and the relatives' resources. The casualty officer stands at the collision point between the patient's need, the family's worries and the hospital's overcrowded beds. How often have I searched a patient for an upturning big toe or a possible mass in the rectum to strengthen the case for admission to a sceptical Registrar, while a knot of relatives, probably now living thirty miles away, cast grave looks.

There has long been concern about the poor state of the accident services, which cope with five million accident victims every year. Sir Henry Osmond-Clarke's Review Committee noted 'insufficient and inadequate staff; inadequate accommodation; lack of rehabilitation departments' and generally low priority. One of the members of the working party noted 'Old departments which were dirty and dingy, with patients waiting in corridors, and clean wounds being stitched without any pretence of sterile surgical precautions.' Yet hospital closures mean automatically the permanent loss of casualty stations well able to cope with minor and moderate injury, with correspondingly greater pressure on the remaining units.

Worse still is the position of the ambulance service, which has to cart patients who have pleaded unsuccessfully for admission back to their homes. More and more patients are shuttled about by the ambulance service, and acute admissions in London would be in open crisis if not for the referral work done by the privately funded Emergency Bed Service, itself under financial review, despite creating a new grade of 'hospital practitioner', described by the President of the Royal College of Radiologists as a 'a bad grade. When there is a shortage it is tempting to appoint a pair of hands. I find it difficult to understand why more people are not dismayed', the number of patients who had waited over one year for surgery lengthened by between 10 and 25 per cent between September 1975 and March 1976. And when it is hard to see a doctor, people just do without and pathological disorders which could have been prevented go unattended.

Cuts in general practice

The picture in general practice is hard to evaluate. From all sides come demands that G. P.s should undertake more clinical responsibility. *The Economist* puts the case with its customary cost-effective curtness:

In order to establish an attitude of mind, rather than in the hope of saving very much, the Royal Commission should consider junking, for example, routine school medical examinations (general practitioners should look after their own); the cervical smear campaign (only a small proportion of the 2.3 million women covered are at risk); infant welfare clinics (back to the family doctor again) and so on.[9]

All the projected swing to community care assumes a considerable increase in the work-load of G. P.s. However, district nurses complain that G. P.s hide behind their answering services, while Community Health Councils suspect them of lounging in golf-club bars. The Patients' Association has compiled evidence of 'patients who have been ill for one or two years before any attempt is made to carry out tests. They died within a few months or a few weeks of reaching hospital.' The Association says it is 'worried by the number of people not referred for tests by their doctors'. There is evidence that practice receptionists issue a high proportion of repeat prescriptions without supervision from the doctor. G. P.s still see too many patients for too short a time. An average initial consultation in Harley Street would take half-an-hour, what any M. P. would want and get. Those who vote for them get an average of three minutes.

These shortcoming are inevitable when hospital administrators, as in Queen Elizabeth's Hospital for Sick Children in Bethnal Green, have to insist on 'stopping or severely curtailing supportive services such as pathological investigations' and the Area Health Authority in the same region proposes that 'a lower priority should be given to G. P. referral services for X-ray and pathology; requests for investigations must be authorised by a Consultant or Senior Registrar', when GPs are paid according to a complex system of service fees for screening, and health centres, from which effective night cover can be provided which would ease night admissions to hospital, have just ceased building. British G. P.s are still weighed down with issuing certificates for sickness absence, often for the most trivial illnesses but required by personnel authorities at work. In Holland there is a separate cadre of insurance doctors who have no permanent clinical responsibilities. In Sweden workers are trusted to declare themselves for the first week, with occasional checks by sick fund officers.

One G. P. at the B. M. A. Representative Meeting in March 1977 said the problems were 'lack of resources, incomes policy and the open-ended commitment of the profession to provide a service without resources' – a long-winded way of saying cuts. It may be the case that the older generation of practitioners have treasured their 'independent contractor' status long after it lost any real meaning. But those who think it is morally improving for a G. P. to attend his own night calls should imagine the pressure, after seeing thirty patients in surgery and doing several home visits, of picking one's way through the mess caused by the cuts, industrial action and the sheer size and inefficiency of our super-hospitals to find the relevant admitting officer, persuading him of the merits of the case only to find there are no available beds, and starting the whole performance with the next hospital, and then having to inform relatives and the ambulance service – all after an interrupted night and with the prospect of another twenty-five evening surgery patients. There is some danger that G. P.s are going to be expected to increase their clinical work-load dramatically, according to the community-based service's new needs, while their financial and material resources actually worsen.

The Department of Health's Chief Medical Officer, Sir Henry Yellowless, has already held crisis meetings with G. P.s' representatives on the state of general practice in the inner-city areas' where there is a real fear that general practice might cease to exist. More than 1000 G. P.s are due to retire in the London area alone in the next five years. In these areas high practice rents, lack of health centres, few training practices and unattractive postgraduate facilities combine with the better-known housing and educational problems to make general practice a very daunting undertaking.

The 'community'

Almost inevitably it will be the woman at home who will end up holding the baby, and the sick uncle or the miscarrying mother. Women campaigners against hospital closures in the Islington Health District wrote:

> The propaganda campaign for 'community care' is very dishonest and mainly aimed at getting the public to accept the rundown of the NHS in the vague belief that other facilities exist. The trick is they don't and community care means that we will have to care for the chronically, but not critically, sick young and old in the home. This can only be done if more and more women stay at home to take on this task. We do not say that only women can care for the

sick but we expect that in practice this will be what happens. Without much support from either the health service or the local council this could well mean a reversion to the bad old days of imprisonment in the home for many women.

The patients

As for more general impacts of the cuts on medical standards, they will range between simply greater inconvenience for patients, through the withdrawal of known but now overcostly methods of treatment, to the point where medical and nursing standards are stretched so paper thin that tragedy, the unnecessary loss of life, becomes inevitable. It is impossible to evaluate in words or statistics the suffering that will be caused by womb cancer that could be averted by mobile cervical screening units, the death sentence when the administrators simply cease offering renal dialysis facilities to the thousands of young people with serious kidney failure or the silently, inwardly endured misery of children made ugly by progressive curvature of the spine or twisted feet who Mr John Sharrard, the orthopaedic surgeon at Sheffield Children's Hospital, has said will remain untreated because of the long waiting-lists and spending cuts. As for the steadily rising rates of both whooping cough and poliomyelitis, there is a danger we will only find out what is really the cause – lower vaccination rates, poorer child health services or worsening domestic hygiene – when a big epidemic finally brings the problems out into the open. However, ignorance cannot be an excuse in the case of our child health services, in a fragmented and inadequate state with poor uptake of pre-natal care and uneven provision for those children most in need. A veritable holocaust still haunts the working-class new-born. Professor S. D. M. Court's massive inquiry documents the tragedy whereby 'children still die in our lifetime of nineteenth century reasons'.[10] The problem is that the government has accepted the report, with its call for a general practitioner paediatrician grade to replace the present school and clinic doctors (mostly married women working on a part-time basis), in principle. They will then, as the B. M. A. puts it, 'begin a morale-damaging dismantling of the present structure without the finance or the will to begin building the new one'. Macabrely the N. H. S. charge for the burial of a still-born child has increased from £8 to £14.30. The death grant remains at £9.

The medical professions' reaction as one after another of these

ambitious schemes bite the dust is likely to become 'better the
mediocrity we know than the utopias that never arrive'. One lengthy
study, sympathetic to the general aims of the D. H. S. S. community-
based plans, in *Priorities for Health and Personal Social Services in
England*, concluded that, 'the consultative document has turned out
to be nothing more than a smokescreen for ever-increasing public
expenditure cuts', and adds, 'Most important, the cuts will merely
reduce the services in their existing shape, and will definitely not
change their emphasis and structure.'

Women

There are other fields where pointers can be seen relating to the risks
brought about by cuts in the health service. Especially marked effects
are being felt in obstetrics, geriatrics and psychiatry. The Royal
College of Physicians, not usually a radical body, has warned
explicitly against the repercussions that the closure of obstetric beds,
justified by the falling birth rate, will have on medical facilities for
women in general:

> Under the present plan the obstetric services are to suffer the most
> stringent cuts. It is likely, because of the effect that this will have on
> staffing and recruitment, that facilities for gynaecology will also be
> curtailed. If this is so the gynaecology waiting lists, already among
> the longest, will lengthen still further. Already nearly a quarter of
> all women admitted for perineal repair have waited six months or
> more.[11]

Cuts justified by very vague references to falling birth rates have
especially affected the G. P.-run obstetric units, which combine the
safety of hospital delivery with the homeliness of domestic child-
birth, have increased the distances and often the waits for pre-natal
clinics, key factors in women's ability to attend, and exaggerated a
tendency toward day-time delivery. Staffing pressure rather than
innate sadism is the cause of impersonal care, overhasty inductions
and unnecessary episiotomies, resented by more and more women –
and men – who want to take an active and informed part in birth.
But pence rather than pleasure is the rule. The night staff often come
on duty exhausted after a day with their own children, the houseman
is half-asleep, and the material pressures of an overstressed system,
however hard a liberal-minded consultant tries, still pushes to the

limits the patient's capacity for submission and their attendants' capacity for insensitivity.

The conflict between home *versus* hospital delivery has arisen because such pressure is placed on the hospitals they cannot help becoming so mechanical that it is considered a great thing to do something that ought to be basic, like delivering the baby straight into the mother's arms. And this will get worse as facilities contract. As Professor Richard Beard of St Mary's Hospital put it: 'The big danger that worried obstetricians have is that all the things we have achieved – a low perinatal mortality and safety for the mother in pregnancy – will be endangered by an unthinking attitude to savings.'[12] Although the birth rate has fallen for several years, projections by the Government Office Population Censuses and Surveys indicate that the number of births will start to increase in 1977 and continue to increase for a further ten years.

The old

In the geriatric field it is now often the case that concern for community facilities makes it harder than ever for an older person to be admitted to the acute beds which are being cut so dramatically in their name. Leicester Age Concern compiled a dossier on a 77-year-old widow, so ill that all she could do was sit in a chair, not even feed herself, but who had been refused hospital admission for eighteen months. As the local Age Concern spokesman put it: 'The social services departments and the hospitals just pass the buck backwards and forwards and it's getting worse because of the cutbacks.' There are thousands of women who, awaiting pneumonia, unvisited, ill-fed and unhappy, are victims of a society which can keep them alive but not give them a life worth living. And even where elderly patients can get a place in a geriatric ward, there is little relief from their isolation and boredom. Geriatric patients in long-stay wards are clean and well-fed but often sit all day in high-backed chairs with nothing to do. An increase in the geriatric service has occurred despite the cuts but only too often in all geriatric units rather than part of general hospitals.

Psychiatry

Even more marked is the decline in psychiatric care. The closure of the custodial asylums, fired by humanitarian motives, has resulted in more and more badly disturbed patients, who are supposed to be under 'community care' but who, in the absence of adequate hostels, sheltered homes, day hospitals and staff, exist between intramuscular injections of tranquillisers, industrial retraining units, which are little better than workhouses, and the mercies of the police. The ill-treatment and neglect which still occurs regularly in the understaffed, overcrowded wards of the large mental hospitals are expensive to remedy. After the St Augustine's scandal an emergency panel recommended changes which would have cost £1.4 million. In fact only £112,000 could be found, and a year after the inquiry conditions had worsened in some instances. Nor is the situation of the psychiatric wings of general hospitals, which were meant to take over from the asylums, much better. Psychiatrists in the Hackney Hospital, a wing of St Bart's teaching unit, reported:

The wards have no curtains around the beds, so there is no privacy for patients at all. Every type of patient is treated together – the young, aged, dementing, violent, depressed. More than 50 families or individuals arrive every week in acute distress for first aid from the duty psychiatrist, who can only admit those in danger of killing themselves, or someone else. There are no services at all for accommodating severely disturbed children or adolescents, nor any hostels. Junior doctors are forced to see one out-patient every ten minutes.

The effects of the cuts can be seen in everything from research into blood disease, cervical cancer and haemophilia to the striking current decline in dental standards which took decades to build up. The Royal College of Physicians comments:

The most harmful effect of the cuts that are envisaged is that they may prevent, or bring to a halt, special developments of great potential value to the Health Service but which are not yet ready for general application. This levelling down of some of the most advanced centres of research and postgraduate training may well have wide repercussions on the standard of the service as a whole.

The D. H. S. S. has announced cuts in medical facilities in the event of an H-bomb exploding. In a nuclear war most people would have to wait days or weeks for medical attention, and those suffering only from radiation sickness would have to fend for themselves. Even the end of the world is now under-budgeted.

Further reading

Brian Abel-Smith, *The Hospitals 1800–1948* (London: Heinnemann, 1964).

Danny Abse, *Medicine on Trial* (London: Aldus, 1967).

K. Coates and R. Silburn, *Poverty: the Forgotten Englishman* (Harmondsworth: Penguin, 1970).

Vernon Coleman, *The Medicine Man* (London: Temple Smith, 1975).

Barbara Ehrenreich and Deidre English, *Complaints and Disorders: The Sexual Politics of Sickness* (London: Writers and Readers Publishing Cooperative, 1976).

Barbara Ehrenreich and Deidre English, *Witches, Midwives and Nurses: A History of Women Healers* (London: Writers and Readers Publishing Cooperative 1976).

Michael Foot, *Aneurin Bevan*, vol. 1 (London: McGibbon and Kee Ltd, 1962), vol. 2 (London: Davis-Poynter, 1973).

Paul Foot, *Stop the Cuts* (London: Rank and File Centre, 1976).

George Godber, *The British National Health Service* (Washington, D.C.: U.S. Department of Health, Education and Welfare, 1976).

Haslemere Group and War on Want, *Who Needs the Drug Companies?* (Birmingham: Third World Publications, 1976).

Tom Heller, *Poor Health, Rich Profits* (Nottingham: Spokesman Books, 1977).

Hospital Worker, bi-monthly (available from 78 Edith Grove, London SWIO).

Ivan Illich, *Medical Nemesis* (London: Calder and Boyars, 1975).

International Journal of Health Services, quarterly (Baywood Publishing Company, John Hopkins University, Baltimore).

J. C. Kincaid, *Poverty and Inequality in Britain* (Harmondsworth: Penguin, 1973).

Patrick Kinnersley, *The Hazards of Work* (London: Pluto Press, 1973).

Alan Klass, *There's Gold in them thar Pills* (Harmondsworth: Penguin, 1975).

Nancy Mackeith, *Women's Health Handbook* (London: Virago, 1978).

Medicine in Society, quarterly (available from 16 King Street, London WC2).

Vincent Navarro, *Medicine and Capitalism* (London: Croom Helm, 1977).

Vincent Navarro, *Class Struggle, The State, and Medicine* (London: Martin Robertson, London 1978).

David Owen, *In Sickness and in Health* (London: Quartet, 1976).

Radical Statistics Health Group, *In Defence of the N. H. S.* (London, 1977).

John Robson, *Quality, Inequality and Health Care* (London: Marxists in Medicine, 1976).

John Robson, *Take a Pill . . . The Drug Industry, Private or Public* (London: Marxists in Medicine, 1976).

Michael Rose, *The Relief of Poverty 1834–1914* (London: Macmillan, 1972).

M. Sissons and P. French (eds), *The Age of Austerity* (Harmondsworth: Penguin 1964).

Socialist Worker, weekly (available from Cambridge Crescent, Cambridge Heath Road, London E2).

Gareth Stedman Jones, *Outcast London* (Oxford University Press, 1971).

The Hospital Worker's Almanac (London: Hospital Worker, 1977 – available from 19 Red Post Hill, London SE23).

Julian Tudor Hart *The National Health Service in England and Wales: A Marxist Perspective* (London: Marxists in Medicine, 1976).

J. Westergaard and H. Resler, *Class in a Capitalist Society* (Harmondsworth: Penguin, 1976).

Elizabeth Wilson, *Women and the Welfare State* (London: Tavistock, 1977).

Jock Young and Victoria Greenwood, with a foreword by Peter J. Huntingford, *Abortion in Demand* (London: Pluto Press, 1976).

References

Chapter 1

1. C. Newman, *The Evolution of Medical Education in the Nineteenth Century* (Oxford University Press, 1957) p. 59. Cited in Brian Abel-Smith, *The Hospitals 1800–1948* (London: Heinemann, 1964).
2. Charles Brook, *Carlile and the Surgeons* (Glasgow: Strickland Press, 1945). I owe this reference to Ken Weller.
3. E. P. Thompson, *The Making of the English Working Class* (Harmondsworth: Penguin, 1974) p. 295.
4. R. A. Lewis, *Edwin Chadwick and the Public Health Movement 1832–38* (London: Longman, 1952). Cited in John Robson, *Quality, Inequality and Health Care* (London: Marxists in Medicine, 1976).
5. Frances Cobbe, 'The Sick Poor in Workhouses', *Journal of the Workhouse Visiting Society*, 1861, p. 487. Cited in Abel-Smith, *The Hospitals 1800–1948*.
6. Commission Report, *Lancet*, 1866, p. 34.
7. Robert Roberts, *The Classic Slum* (Harmondsworth: Penguin, 1973) pp. 102–29.
8. Mrs Layton, *Life As We Have Known It* (London: Women's Co-operative Guild) p. 8. Reprinted by Virago (London, 1977).
9. Robert Roberts, *The Classic Slum*, p. 108.
10. Danny Abse, *Medicine on Trial* (London: Aldus, 1967) p. 12.
11. *Hospital*, 26 April 1890, vol. xxvIII, p. 43. Cited in Abel-Smith, *The Hospitals 1800–1948*.
12. S. and B. Webb, *The Poor Law Medical Officer and his Future* (London, 1909).
13. S. and B. Webb, Report of the Royal Commission on the Poor Laws 1905–9, *Minority Report*.
14. Report of the Royal Commission on the Poor Laws 1905–9, Appendix.
15. Charles Chaplin, *My Autobiography* (London: Bodley Head, 1964).
16. S. and B. Webb, *Our Partnership* (London: Longman, 1948) p. 342.

17. Benjamin Moore, 'Society for a State Medical Service'. Cited in D. S. Murray, *Why an NHS?* (London: Pemberton, 1972) p. 6.

Chapter 2

1. Wal Hannington, *The Problem of the Distressed Areas* (London: Gollancz, 1937) p. 57.
2. Cited in G. D. M. and M. Cole, *The Condition of Britain* (London: Gollancz, 1938) p. 101.
3. Cited in Peter Jenkins, 'Beven's Fight with B. M. A.' in M. Sissons and P. French (eds), *The Age of Austerity* (Harmondsworth: Penguin, 1964) pp. 240–66.
4. See Michael Foot, *Aneurin Bevan*, vol. 2 (London: Davis-Poynter, 1973) pp. 100–26.
5. Ibid.
6. D. S. Murray, *Why an NHS?* (London: Pemberton, 1972).

Chapter 3

1. Michael Kidron, *Western Capitalism since the War* (Harmondsworth: Pelican, 1970) p. 11.
2. C. A. R. Crosland, *The Future of Socialism* (London: Cape, 1956).
3. K. Coates and R. Silburn, *Poverty: The Forgotten Englishman* (Harmondsworth: Penguin, 1970) p. 14.
4. Richard Titmuss, *Commitment to Welfare* (London: Unwin, 1968).
5. David Ennals, speech to the Socialist Medical Association, reproduced in *Labour Monthly*, July 1977.
6. See John Robson, *Quality, Inequality and Health Care* (London: Marxists in Medicine, 1976) especially pp. 41–9.
7. Cited in Jonathan Steele, 'How U. S. doctors bleed the government', *Guardian*, 30 August 1976.
8. Antony Holden, 'The horrors and glories of American medicine', *Sunday Times*, 11 March 1973.
9. Richard Crossman, *The Crossman Diaries* (London: Weidenfeld and Nicolson, 1977).
10. Hospital Advisory Service Annual Report 1969–70 (London: H. M. S. O.).
11. *Design*, September 1975, no. 321, p. 60.
12. See Kennedy Cruickshank, 'Who becomes doctors?', *New Society*, 15 January 1976, p. 112.
13. Titmuss, *Commitment to Welfare*.
14. Bethnal Green Trades Council, *A People's Health Service for Tower Hamlets* (1975) p. 12.

Chapter 4

1. J. S. Collings, 'General Practice – England Today', *Lancet*, 1950, p. 555.
2. A. Cartwright and J. Marshall, 'General Practice in 1963', *Medical Care*, 1965, p. 69.

Chapter 5

1. A. Watt, 'Overcrowding in the Mental Hospital', *Lancet*, 1956.
2. Cited in G. L. Cohen, *What's Wrong with Hospitals?* (Harmondsworth: Penguin, 1964).
3. Jack Tizard, *Community Services for the Mentally Handicapped* (Oxford University Press, 1964).
4. See J. A. Baldwin, *The Mental Hospital in the Psychiatric Service* (Oxford University Press, 1971).

Chapter 6

1. D. H. S. S., *Priorities for Health and Personal Services in England* (London: H. M. S. O., 1976).
2. *Lancet*, 1959, p. 584.
3. Monopolies Commission, *A Report on the Supply of Chlordiazepoxide and Diazepam*, HCP197 (London: H. M. S. O., 1973).
4. *British Medical Journal*, 23 July 1977, p. 240.

Chapter 7

1. Cited in Robson, *Quality, Inequality and Health Care*.
2. *Hospital Worker*, no. 4, p. 3.
3. Esther Brookstone, *Medicine in Society*, vol. 2, no. 1, p. 2.
4. Cited in R. Rappaport, 'A Candle for St Greeds', *Harper's Magazine*, December 1972.
5. *The Times*, 16 December 1975.

Chapter 8

1. *Backlash*, December 1972, no. 1.
2. *Hospital Worker*, May 1974 (Nurses' Special).
3. *Hospital Worker*, July 1974.
4. *Hospital Worker*, August 1974.
5. *Western Daily Press*, 19 August 1974, p. 6.
6. *The Economist*, 25 October 1975.
7. *Guardian*, 13 December 1975. For an excellent survey of the juniors' dispute see Harvey Gordon and Steve Iliffe, *Pickets in White* (London: M. P. U. Publications, 1977).

Chapter 9

Detailed citations for this chapter can be found in *Paying for the Crisis* and *Cutting the Welfare State*, both reports from Counter Intelligence Services; *Labour Monthly*; and Gerry Dawson's survey 'What's happening to the N. H. S.?', *International Socialism*, June 1977, no. 99.

1. Peter Jay in *The Times*, 20 February 1976.
2. *Business Week*, 29 March 1976.
3. *The Economist*, 28 June 1975.
4. Cmnd. 6721 (London: H. M. S. O., 1976).
5. *Investors' Chronicle*, 11 September 1974.
6. 'The Financing of the National Health Service' – a joint statement by the B. M. A., B. D. A., J. C. C., R. C. N. and R. C. M., *British Medical Journal*, 2 November 1974.
7. *British Medical Journal*, 27 November 1976, p. 1320.
8. *Women's Voice*, September 1977.
9. *The Economist*, 21 July 1976.
10. *Fit for the Future*, Report of the Committee on the Child Health Service, (London: H. M. S. O., 1976) vols 1, 2.
11. Comments by the Royal College of Physicians of London, *British Medical Journal*, 20 November 1976, p. 1248.
12. *British Medical Journal*, 23 July 1977.